You Are Prosperous!

The
Prosperity Code

How to Find It, Decipher It and Use
It for Permanent Prosperity

Alan Batten

BALBOA.
PRESS
A DIVISION OF HAY HOUSE

Balboa Press books may be ordered through booksellers or by contacting:

Balboa Press
A Division of Hay House
1663 Liberty Drive
Bloomington, IN 47403
www.balboapress.com
1-(877) 407-4847

Because of the dynamic nature of the Internet, any web addresses or links contained in this book may have changed since publication and may no longer be valid. The views expressed in this work are solely those of the author and do not necessarily reflect the views of the publisher, and the publisher hereby disclaims any responsibility for them.

The author of this book does not dispense medical advice or prescribe the use of any technique as a form of treatment for physical, emotional, or medical problems without the advice of a physician, either directly or indirectly. The intent of the author is only to offer information of a general nature to help you in your quest for emotional and spiritual well-being. In the event you use any of the information in this book for yourself, which is your constitutional right, the author and the publisher assume no responsibility for your actions.

Any people depicted in stock imagery provided by Thinkstock are models, and such images are being used for illustrative purposes only. Certain stock imagery © Thinkstock.

ISBN: 978-1-4525-5267-5 (sc)
ISBN: 978-1-4525-5269-9 (hc)
ISBN: 978-1-4525-5268-2 (e)

Library of Congress Control Number: 2012910676

Printed in the United States of America
Balboa Press rev. date: 6/18/2012

Also by this author:

Branding TV: Principles and Practices
Focal Press

Dedication

To Scott, Glenn, Shannon,
Bennett and Landon Batten.
My Abundance.

Acknowledgements

My undying appreciation goes to Alannah Joy Johnson,
Velories Anne Figures and Susan Doyle
who reviewed this manuscript and encouraged me.
Thanks also to Imani Chapman for her artistic skills and
Greg James for his lyrics to "Forgive Yourself."

Contents

Dedication   vii

Acknowledgements   ix

Introduction: Why You Need This Book   xiii

Key Number 1: What is Prosperity?   1

Key Number 2: Your Order, Please   5

Key Number 3: It's Not Just a Good Idea, It's a Law!   9

Key Number 4: Seven Steps to Using the Law of Attraction   15

Key Number 5: Faith-You Must Believe   27

Key Number 6: Give, Give, Give   37

Key Number 7: The Secret Missing Link   45

Key Number 8: The Dreaded F Word!   53

Key Number 9: Have a Prosperity State of Mind   61

Key Number 10: Have A Regular Spiritual Practice   67

Key Number 11: Examine And Modify Your Core Values.   73

Solving the Code: Putting it all Together   79

Recommended Reading   85

Afterword   87

Introduction:
Why You Need This Book

E very day and every night, we are bombarded with bits and pieces of code. (No, I'm not talking about putting on a tin foil hat to keep the UFOs out of your brain. This is not that kind of book.) The codes I refer to here are from radio, television, microwave, GPS, cell phones and much more.

All these codes serve us in one way or another, if we know how to receive them and decode them. From the most basic Morse Code to the sophisticated telemetry from the Hubble Space Telescope, all this information is in some kind of code.

But there is an entirely different Code.

It is a secret Code that only a relatively few people have found and deciphered.

Like all secret Codes, it is shrouded in mystery, wrapped in riddles and enclosed in inscrutability.

People have been seeing bits and pieces of this Code for millennia, but many have not grasped the meaning of the diverse parts.

Very few people realize what this Code is and even fewer people know how to use it.

It is the Code which allows dreams to be realized; the Code that opens doors and makes all things possible.

Countless people have been seeking it, but if they find it, they don't have the key to unlock it.

This hard to find and hard to break code is **The Prosperity Code.**

When you take a closer look at its fundamental origins, the history of humankind has been almost wholly taken up with the quest for prosperity. Our earliest ancestors, like all animals on the planet, were constantly questing for food and shelter from the elements. If they had something to eat, they felt prosperous because their bellies were full. If they went hungry, they continued their quest.

As they became more "civilized" over the years, their search for prosperity continued through acquiring more and more of whatever it was that made them feel prosperous. (Even those who called themselves recluses or hermits were seeking their own special form of prosperity with solitude, ashes or sackcloth.)

As soon as we humans are born into this world, we seek prosperity in nourishment, shelter and one of the various forms of love that has developed over the millennia. In our earliest time on this planet, we evolved our skills to be nomadic hunters and gatherers. The group celebrated their prosperity with a feast when the hunters brought home an animal.

As we continued through the eons, we found that we could stay in one place and grow our own form of prosperity with livestock, fruits, vegetables and grains. From that discovery sprang settlements, towns, cities, and nation-states. And conflict ensued.

Wars were started to be won and lost.

Empires were built and toppled.

Quests were undertaken.

Lives were affected.

All in the quest for prosperity.

Jan Van Rijn, an 18th Century Dutch burgher, was judged prosperous because he and his family were what we now call fat or obese. A thin person was derided as a poor person. Having enough resources to overeat was considered an ideal thing. Consuming copious amounts of food, and in the case of the proverbial burgher, having an investment in rare tulip bulbs, were sure signs of prosperity.

Many people tried many things to become prosperous; some worked, most didn't.

Those whose ideas failed inevitably asked themselves: "What is the secret of prosperity? I keep striving for abundance and somehow fall short. Is there some sort of code I can't recognize? What is it? Where do I find it? How do I solve it?"

The Prosperity Code has eluded seekers for centuries. It has mysteriously escaped the clutching hands of those who wanted it the most.

> Prosperity is not just having things. It is the consciousness that attracts the things. Prosperity is a way of living and thinking, and not just having money or things. Poverty is a way of living and thinking, and not just a lack of money or things.
> —Eric Butterworth

Yet, others seemed to have it from the get-go. They had no trouble in manifesting abundance for themselves.

A code is meaningless to those who do not have the key; yet anyone with the key are able to use the code to their advantage.

Do you have the key to the Prosperity Code? Perhaps you know of someone who is very prosperous. Do they have the key to the Code?

We live in a Universe of Abundance. Abundance should be ours for the mere asking. Why do we suffer and strive so hard with so little result?

Countless books have been written about this quest for the key to the Prosperity Code, from Napoleon Hill's *Think and Grow Rich* to the classic series by Catherine Ponder and *The Secret*.

What makes this book any different?

This is not a book of dry, academic discussions of the theory of prosperity and abundance. If you want that, there are many places you can get it. Please pass *this* book along to a friend who wants a practical, workable guide that provides the experience of attracting abundance of all kinds into his or her life.

Designed to bring you into your rightful abundance, this short tome has suggestions and exercises that are easy to understand and follow.

The ideas in this book must, of necessity, have a foundation in the invisible; in the realm of Spirit. You may see Spirit as God, Allah, Buddha, Jesus, Source, The Law of Attraction or even The Great Cosmic Muffin. Your name and concept of the Higher Power is yours to use in this book as you desire.

Why do we have to bring in a Higher Power? As Albert Einstein stated "You cannot solve a problem on the level it was created." So, we're going to kick the search for prosperity *Upstairs*.

This book will give you some simple instructions, or Eleven Keys to the Code, which—if you follow them—will reveal and unlock the Prosperity Code for you and for your life.

This is a big "If". To get the results, you must do the work. Learn the keys to the Code and it will open everything for you.

Perhaps you've heard the old story of the woman who wanted God's help in winning the Mega Millions Jackpot lottery. Every time the jackpot would get over $200 million, she would earnestly pray "God, help me win the lottery."

After many, many years of saying that prayer without the results she desired, she broke down in despair and cried out with a great gnashing of teeth and rending of garments: "God, I've been a good and faithful servant. I don't smoke, I don't drink and I'm very chaste in my relationships. Why, oh why haven't You helped me win the lottery?"

The clouds above broke and a great beam of light hit her, and she heard "Child, help Me out here. Buy a ticket!"

So, unfasten your seatbelt, put down your tray table, turn on your electronic reading device, and get set to become prosperous beyond your wildest dreams.

But help God out here.

Buy a ticket.

Key Number 1:
What is Prosperity?

n order to unlock the Prosperity Code, we must first come up with our own definition of *prosperity*, or *abundance*. It's probably safe to note that there are as many definitions of prosperity as there are people to define it.

I have been facilitating prosperity classes for more than two decades. Some years ago, I conducted a class where I asked my students to come up with a dollar figure at which they would consider themselves prosperous. After some extensive discussion and elimination of any number that included "a billion," the consensus was a relatively modest $500. The class all set this as their goal. They then did much the same work as you will do in this book to realize that figure.

I was conducting the weekly check-in as members of the class shared their prosperity stories some two weeks after we set the goal. We all applauded when someone had a successful event in his or her life over the previous week. I encouraged the class to report even if they found a penny on the sidewalk. Some reported receiving an unexpected amount of money, having a bill paid for them, or discovering a twenty-dollar bill used as a bookmark and forgotten long ago. It was always fun to hear how people found their abundance.

As the check-in time neared its end, one young woman stood up and announced, "I set my goal at $5,000, even though I thought it was out of reach." We all gasped, but she continued. "Today I was called into my supervisor's office. I was scared and wondered if I had done something wrong." She continued with an excited grin on her face, "I was wrong, all right! I was given a raise!" We congratulated her. But she put up a hand.

"Wait!" she cried. "Wait! The raise was for $5,000 a year!" We all went wild with excitement. She beamed and sat down.

And we never saw her again after that night.

To that young woman, her definition of prosperity was $5,000.

For the longest time, my personal definition of prosperity was to make $100,000 a year. A good friend of mine, when I shared my goal with him, said, "Why so low? God thinks you are entitled to more than a million dollars a year! You're limiting yourself!" So I revised *my* definition of prosperity drastically upward.

What's *your* definition?

> You can open your mind to prosperity when you realize the true definition of the word: You are prosperous to the degree you are experiencing peace, health and plenty in your world. —Catherine Ponder

"Prosperity" is more than having the most money, more than having the most shoes, more than having an unending supply of things, and more than dying with the most toys. You can be the richest person in the world in terms of things, yet you can lack any sort of human contact or meaningful relationships.

You can be apparently rich in *things* and impoverished in love. It's true that money can't buy real happiness—when we spend it exclusively on ourselves. (You may want to ask Howard Hughes the next time you're at a séance.)

One working definition of prosperity is being able to do *what* you want, *when* you want, with *whom* you want. This could include taking an exotic vacation to the Greek Isles on a chartered yacht;

going on an unlimited, week-long shopping spree at Neiman-Marcus; or simply being able to take your clothes to the cleaners whenever you wished.

Another definition of prosperity is being able to give an unlimited amount of time and money to worthy causes. This may involve setting up a foundation whose name would be all over PBS. Or you may think of being like one very large player whose company name is a household word around the world, giving funding only on the condition that the company's name would not be revealed.

There is also prosperity of health and well-being. If you have an abundance of peace and harmony, anything else really doesn't matter. We may hear stories of Hindu mystics high in the Himalayas who contemplate infinity for many years. They could care less about the $500 goal of the prosperity class. They may spend their time caring about the natural world, which, of course, was here long before the $500.

> Successful people make money. It's not that people who make money become successful, but that successful people attract money. They bring success to what they do. —Wayne Dyer

As I have noted, financial prosperity is only one aspect of abundance. **Abundance boils down to a sense of well-being.** At any given moment, if you have a good sense of well-being, then you are prosperous and are experiencing abundance, joy, harmony, happiness, and fulfillment.

Think of a time when you felt really prosperous. It could be an early childhood memory when you discovered Santa had left you twenty-eight cents in your Christmas stocking, and you thought you were the richest kid in the world.

Or it could have been a time when you received an unexpected check or bonus and you decided to treat yourself and a loved one to a night on the town. It might be right after you moved into a new house, working at a new job, driving a company car, and living large on an expense account.

Abundance is often used interchangeably with prosperity. Abundance is a "gracious plenty" of the good things in life, as people would say in the Southern United States.

John Randolph Price defines abundance as "an all-sufficiency of supply, a full measure of infinite good. In the invisible, it is the creative energy of God In the visible world, it is that energy made manifest as money and every other food thing required for a free and harmonious life."

What's your vision of prosperity?

If you don't have a good working definition of prosperity, how are you going to know it when you get it?

Now, here's your chance to write in a book. Unless it is a library copy or an e-book, you can write your definition of prosperity right here. Take as much time as you need and as much space as you want (on an additional piece of paper) to write your definition. You will come back to it during the course of reading this book when you wish to modify and expand it.

It could be as simple as "I am prosperous when I can go out to eat six nights a week at great restaurants." Or it could be "I am prosperous when I can take my car to the car wash whenever it gets dusty." It can be as complex as "I am prosperous when I can take my family on a month-long, first-class trip to China and have a great time regardless of the cost."

So please fill in the blank.

I feel prosperous when _____ .

How does being prosperous make you *feel?* I know that's the dreaded *f* word. But one day, you've got to get in touch with your feelings, especially if you want the techniques in this book to work for you.

Hold on to the memory of that feeling; you will need it later in this book.

Key Number 2:
Your Order, Please

You have pulled up to the Universe's Drive Through Window, and the voice in the speaker says "Your order, please."

Are you going to order the same stuff you usually order? "Yeah," you say, "give me a helping of anxiety, some seasoned wretchedness, and a supersized cup of despair!"

"Ah, the usual!" says the voice. "We have a special going today: a heaping portion of unworthiness at no extra charge. Please pull ahead to the next window." So the Universe hands you more anxiety, wretchedness, and despair. Plus, a huge free helping of uselessness. With salted fries. And you are glad.

That's a simplification of how your life may have been going—up until now. You are getting exactly what you ordered.

"But," say you, "I didn't order that!"

I beg to differ.

At some deep level, you did.

The concept of taking personal responsibility for your life is one that is probably foreign to you. All your life you have believed that you were affected by the world out there. You

> Every thought we think is creating our future.
> —Louise L. Hay

believed that you have no more power over the course of your life than does a feather in the wind.

That sort of thinking is a mistake.

And mistakes, as noted in *A Course in Miracles*, are to be corrected, not punished.

That's one of the reasons why you are reading this book, or attending a class or seminar based on this material. You are going to find much of your present thinking challenged, and if you want to be prosperous, you will find that sort of thinking will need to be changed.

Here's a shocker for you: At some level, buried deep in your subconscious, you may truly believe that you are only worthy of worry and woe. You may have received an early massive injection of guilt. Somehow, you may have the idea that you were unworthy of abundance and prosperity.

Wouldn't you like to change that message?

Then crack the Prosperity Code and change your mind-set.

What's Your Mind-Set?

Your mind-set is your way of thinking about anything. It is the baseline for all your thoughts. It is from your mind-set that all your conscious and unconscious thoughts spring.

Your mind-set dictates the colors and flavors of your thoughts. Your mind-set is what tells you your place in your universe. Your mind-set is happily inhabited by your ego, which, by the way, hates change.

Take a look at *your* mind-set.

Do you have a scarcity mind-set or an abundance mind-set?

Someone with a scarcity mind-set sounds a lot like Daffy Duck at his most possessively manic: "It's mine! Do you hear me? It's all mine! Mine! MINE!" In the scarcity mindset, you create fear, desperation, depression, and anxiety. You are stuck in the rut of lack and limitation

> It's God's will for you to live in prosperity instead of poverty. It's God's will for you to pay your bills and not be in debt. —Joel Osteen

with no hope of ever digging your way out. In fact, the scarcity mind-set loves to dig deeper into your pond-scum filled reservoir of fears, frights, frets, and anxieties.

Resembling an out-of-control hoarder on one of those reality TV shows, you keep things you think are valuable. Before you realize it, you are trapped by all that "stuff" and negative thinking. "Never can tell when you will need a piece of string, can you?" asks the scarcity mind-set. "And save that rubber band with the thousands of others in your collection," it implores. Your scarcity mind-set believes the universe will take away everything if you don't hang on to it.

On the other hand, a person with an abundance mind-set knows deep down that the Universe is a place of giving, not taking. An abundance mind-set sees opportunities where others may not. An abundance mind-set sees life with a long-term outlook. Your abundance mind-set knows that your life is filled with opportunities and promise. And, yes cliché fans, that glass is half full.

What kind of mind-set do you have?

It's OK to acknowledge it. We're all friends here. What happens in this book stays in your note book, until the changes we are undertaking work their way into your sub-consciousness and then into your life.

After spending decades in the marketing industry, I observed that the Western-oriented mind is heavily stimulated by marketing. **Marketing is the technique used to convince people that they need something they didn't know they needed.** And they need it *now.* For example, men did not know that they could not live without a safety razor until King Gillette started giving the razors away, but charged for the blades.

It is interesting to note that our Western society is built on the scarcity mind-set. Pay conscious (versus unconscious) attention to advertising, and you will see carefully crafted examples of scarcity mind-set thinking. For example, you won't be popular unless you have the right underarm deodorant. Or people will hate you if you don't drive a particular kind of car, eat a certain kind of food or wear a specific type of makeup or hair dye.

Your children will be at a huge disadvantage unless they drink a particular brand of soda, eat a special cereal and wear the right clothes. Your beloved pet will have a stunted life unless you buy a special kind of food or toy or litter. Unless you have been friended by several thousand total strangers on your social network, you don't count.

How will you survive, your subconscious wonders, with all this lack and limitation? We must do something, says the scarcity mind-set.

Don't sit here, go out and buy something! Buy that underarm deodorant or coffee or cereal to be popular and loved and adored by thousands of people. (And, as an aside, be like everyone else, keeping up with the Joneses.)

Looking at the nightly news or listening to talk radio will also convince your subconscious that the world is going straight to Hell very quickly in a particularly grubby hand-basket. So, it urges you to do something about it: go out and buy a special antacid or luxury SUV and all will be well.

Well, at least the ride to Hell will be comfortable.

With a scarcity mind-set, mistakes are a *Big Deal.* The sky is in danger of crashing down on your head if you make even the smallest error. Punishment is right around the corner for even thinking of making the most minor infraction.

Can you identify with any of the above statements? Do you feel a sense of familiarity with any of the above? Your conscious mind may say not, but I'm betting that your subconscious mind is saying "You Betchya!"

When you change your Mind-set from Scarcity to Abundance, the world will change for you.

To change your way of life, change your way of thinking.

But first, you should study a little Law.

Key Number 3:
It's Not Just a Good Idea, It's a Law!

W e don't only live in a society of laws, we live in a whole *Universe* of Laws. These Laws are often referred to as Laws of Nature, Universal Laws or Spiritual Laws. We are not referring to physical laws such as the law of gravity; we're referring to laws that transcend and often trump the physical laws. Everything in the universe is affected by these principles.

This includes you.

And your vision of abundance.

There are many spiritual rules which cause you to live the life you live, and to know them is to unlock another portion of the Prosperity Code. There are many Universal Laws. Here are a select few for your consideration:

The Law of Oneness With All.

We are all One. We are the diverse parts of Source, all seeking to have our own experiences of good with Source. What happens to one of us affects all of us.

To understand this concept, we have to acknowledge that we actually operate on two planes or levels:

> Remember where your heart is, for there is your treasure also.—*A Course in Miracles*

the Physical, or Earthly plane and in Spirit, or Heavenly plane. We have our experiences of Source in two places: in the Physical plane, and in the Spirit plane. When we finish our experience on the Physical plane, we make our transition to the Spirit plane. This is where we evaluate our progress in achieving the goals we set for ourselves during the physical sojourn. Back home in the Spiritual plane, we set our goals for our next journey to the planetary plane.

The Law of Karma and Reincarnation.

This law essentially states that when you incur any kind of debt, you have to pay it back with interest. Here, I refer not to the debt on the credit card or to the mortgage company or the Student Loan program. I am referring to a debt which you incur to others which has little or no basis in things monetary. Remember, our actual Home is in the Spirit plane; we only visit the Physical plane (aka Earth) to work out problems or to help others work out their problems.

While having experiences on the Physical plane, we often become distracted from our goals because we will have forgotten them. These distractions may cause us to seemingly hurt someone or something we hold dear. If we have not agreed with the other soul prior to returning to the planetary plane that it was our duty to cause hurt, we will gather karmic debt. **This debt may be discharged while still in the body through reconciliation, forgiveness and good deeds. If it is not, we will return to the physical with an obligation of karma to the other soul that we must discharge.**

Again, we will have no memory of this karmic obligation because we have been given a dose of spiritual amnesia so we can discover our paths for ourselves, without a crib sheet.

The Law of Reflection.

The world without is a reflection of the world within. You may be familiar with the saying "As above, so below." What appears without is what has been found within. In the world within may be found infinite Wisdom, infinite Power, infinite Supply of all that is necessary, waiting for development and expression. **If we recognize**

these potentialities in the world within, they will take form in the world without. Most of us live in the world without; only a few of us have found the world within, and yet it is our world within that makes our world without. That is why life is lived from the inside out.

The Law of Abundance.

We live in a Universe of Abundance. Everything and anything in the universe can be ours for the asking. The universe creates it to order. Everything which you find in your world without has been created by you in the world within. **Inner thoughts of Abundance result in outer Abundance.** Thoughts of lack result in outer manifestations of lack. As you think, so it is.

The Law of Cause and Effect.

Every action we take, no matter how small or trifling, has ramifications. If we sow disharmony in our world, this law returns disharmony blessed and multiplied. If we sow peace and love in our world, this law likewise blesses and multiplies peace and harmony. There are no accidents or coincidences. **Everything happens for a reason, even if we have no idea what that reason may be.**

The Law of Higher Vibrations.

We all have the power within us to change our lives, even if we cannot see that power. Simply moving our thoughts to a higher level will change the baser thoughts and move them as well. Everything in creation has its own vibration. Thoughts and rocks, leaves and chipmunks, apples and atoms, humans and stars, all have their own vibration. **Everything is energy in a different form of vibration.** Few people, for example, realize that a pane of glass is actually fluid but at a very slow vibration. Ice is steam at a lower vibration. By moving our thoughts of lack and limitation to a higher vibration, we *will* change our lives.

The Law of Action.

If we wish to have Abundance in our lives, we can't only sit back in our La-Z-Boy chair and hope that the winning letter from the state lottery commission will be delivered by an owl flying down the chimney. **We must take actions that support our thoughts, words, desires and dreams.** See the next chapter on the Seven Steps to The Law of Attraction for more examples of how you can work with this law.

The Law of Instruction.

All Creation is our classroom. We are here to learn. We will have tests and problems to solve. Solving these problems will strengthen and nurture the spark of Source within. This law ties in with the law of karma, and karma—or lack of it—will be our grade. The lack of a karmic debt is known as Wisdom. In this classroom, a test isn't about what you got wrong. It is about what you got right. **When facing thoughts of lack and limitation, think of them as a test and work to overcome them in ways you may not have considered.**

The Law of Free Will.

Even though we have a chance to learn our lessons by following the lesson plan in the classroom of Creation, we have been given a special gift by our Creator: *Free Will.* We can and do change our minds often to either enhance or to alleviate any test we have set up. We have free will in how we respond to any situation. **When life is**

Sometimes we begin at the wrong end of the prosperity line, and our methods need changing. Perhaps we try to accumulate money to meet our temporal needs without first laying hold of the equivalent of money on the inner planes of consciousness. This inner equivalent consists of our rich ideas, our innate capabilities and resources of Spirit.— Myrtle Fillmore

lived from the inside out, free will allows us to respond to our tests with positive feelings, emotions and honor.

The Law of Creation.

Everything starts as a thought. Your food, computer, outfit, car and house all started out as thoughts and variations on those thoughts. You started out as a thought in the mind of at least one of your parents. There is an enormous difference between simply thinking, and directing our thoughts consciously, systematically and constructively to achieve our desires. Thoughts become beliefs and beliefs turn into your own special brand of reality. If you believe that you can only drive a red car, that belief becomes your reality when you purchase or rent only red cars. **To change your reality, you must first change your thoughts, which in turn will change your beliefs.**

The Law of Resistance Persistence.

This law states that what you resist will persist in your life. If you resist your body type, you will continue to experience it. **Since resistance is a form of fear, this law states that you will overcome it by experiencing it.** I have had several examples of this in my classes:

A young Protestant Dutch woman went through a regression experience and discovered that her affinity for Jews and all things Judaic was based on her most recent lifetime when she died as a Jewish prisoner in a Nazi concentration camp.

An African-American man was shocked to discover a lifetime as a merciless slave trader. Many of his current friends in the black community were also his white friends in his 17th Century slave trading company.

An American Air Force veteran with a fondness for the history of the second World War, found that he was a tank driver in the German North Africa Corps in World War II and was killed instantly when an American bomber dropped a bomb into his open tank hatch. He later met a woman whose father was proud of the fact that he had bombed and destroyed a tank in North Africa in 1942.

A young woman hated her body image. Yet, no matter how she tried, she could not change it. She worked with diet after diet, supplement after supplement, exercise program after exercise program. Finally, after spiritual counseling, she came to accept it as her own. After that breakthrough, her body image began to gradually change. Today her body is what she wanted all along.

When you fear something, go through it, don't push it away. You will come out the other side as a stronger, better individual.

The Law of Attraction.

Where your attention goes, your energy flows. Within you is everything you need to manifest Abundance. Also within you is everything you need to experience lack. **What will you attract to yourself?** It is our attitude of mind toward life which determines our experiences; if we expect nothing, we will have nothing; if we demand much, we will receive a larger portion. We are magnets and magnets have an attractive as well as a repulsive pole. How are you oriented? Are you in an attractive mode to attract all things good? Or are you in the repulsive mode which repulses all things good and inversely attracts lack and limitation?

When you are well grounded in the purpose of your life, when you have clarity about your goals and desires and are completely focused on your goals, then God/Source/the Universe will see to your needs.

As stated above, The Law of Attraction very simply states, "Thoughts held in mind bring forth fruit of their own kind." Or as one minister bluntly put it: "My behind follows my mind!"

Whole books and seminars have been based on this simple concept. Esther and Jerry Hicks have a huge library on the Law of Attraction. A simple Internet search will bring you millions of hits about this Law.

Isn't it about time to do something about it in your life?

Or, more properly, isn't it about time to *be* something about it?

Then let's use the Law of Attraction.

Key Number 4:
Seven Steps to Using the
Law of Attraction

Many people are focused on finding a step-by-step solution to their challenges. That is why popular magazines have discovered that they always sell more copies at the news stand when they use a headline that has a number of steps in it. Examples may be "11 Steps to Losing Weight" or "Nine Steps to Finding Your Next Home."

Not to be outdone, I hereby offer Seven Simple Steps will help you go far in unlocking the Code.

This simple "How To Use The Law of Attraction" guide includes:

"Create"
"Focus"
"Act"
"Move"
"Let Go"
"Give Thanks"
"Receive"

Create a conscious intention of what it is you desire.

Start by making a list of your desires.

You may wish to do as I did some years ago. My home was acutely in need of maintenance. The exterior paint was faded and the wood siding had started to deteriorate. The gutters had rotten sections and weren't working well. The wooden fence around my back yard had tragically succumbed to voracious termites. The flooring in the kitchen and bathrooms was in need of an update. The appliances belonged in a Smithsonian exhibit labeled "Antique Excessive Energy Consumers." The central HVAC system operated haphazardly and ingested great gobs of costly electricity.

There were some 16 items I wrote down on the back of an advertising flyer I picked up out of my mailbox. I knew I would like to have these items repaired or replaced. I put the list up on my refrigerator where I could see it every day. Then I let it go so the Universe could work on it without my interference.

Two years passed. One day the list caught my eye again and I sat down at the kitchen table with it. First item: exterior paint and repair: Check! Back yard fence repaired: Check! Kitchen and bathroom floors replaced: Check! New Gutters: Check! New appliances: Check! New dual fuel four-stage energy efficient HVAC unit: Check!

Out of the 16 items on my list, 14 were completed. (I'm still waiting on my interior painting to materialize and some new carpet to be installed.) Simply putting it out to the Universe brought me the wherewithal to have my list virtually completed.

Now, you ask, "Am I going to have to wait two years for my Abundance?"

The answer is a resounding "No!" You can do it much more quickly and efficiently with focus.

Focus on how real it is with a Vision Board.

Take your list and make yourself a "Vision Board" also known as a "Treasure Map." A vision board is a pictorial representation of your prosperity. This board will help kick start your Abundance Mind-set thinking. Like the list of projects I put up on the refrigerator for my subconscious to see every day, your vision board provides you with specific images of what you consider to be prosperity.

> Concentrate on the things you want, not on the things you do not want. Think of abundance; idealize the methods and plans for putting the Law of Abundance into operation. Visualize the condition which the Law of Abundance creates—this will result in manifestation. –Charles Haanel, The Master Key System

Start with a stack of magazines and catalogs which have pictures or illustrations and some scissors. If you don't have a 3x4' board, go to the art or hobby shop and get some sturdy illustration board.

Anyone familiar with scrapbooking will have no problem with what comes next. (Hint: if you have children, enlist their help. They are amazing at finding the perfect images and they love to cut things out.)

Go through the magazines and catalogs and cut out pictures which appeal to your sense of prosperity. If you don't have any magazines, go to a search engine's image bank and look there. Print them out (preferably in color) and put them on the board.

You don't have to limit yourself to tangible things such as a new car or house or vacation. You can also put up images of a great relationship, a comfortable working environment or a secure retirement.

Although making a vision board can be free-form, here is the one *must* to go on it, as close to the center as possible: A representation of Source. **Whatever image appeals to your concept of Source, it must be in the center of your board. It is from Source that all things flow. Acknowledge that in your vision board.**

One other hint: divide your vision board into the various areas of your life: Family, Relationships, Home, Work, Relaxation and Special Projects. A special project may be finishing and submitting the Great American Screenplay or being accepted to an Ivy League College on a full scholarship.

Hang your vision board where you will see it every day. My board is in my office. I urge you to put it where you will be the primary viewer and not in a public space. **Keep your vision board private.** Why? Because if you put it where others who don't share your vision can see and comment upon it, you risk absorbing their negative comments and disparagement. They may say things such as, "You want that? You know that's not for the likes of you!"

Other people may have not gone through the same steps as you have. Your path is unique and so is your vision board. Keep your goals close to your heart, unless you developed them as a family project.

Look at your vision board every day. Take in the totality of the images as well as the individual pictures. Send your board your *positive* thoughts and prayers. A good schedule is upon arising and immediately before retiring. This helps your subconscious entrain the images and work with Source to make them real.

In addition to using your mental and physical vision, you can also enlist your kinesthetic sense, along with your senses of smell, hearing and your imagination.

Depending on your goal, you may focus on the feel of the beach sand under your toes or the smell of the fresh mountain air or the excitement of a major metropolitan area or the quiet of a world class museum. Focus on your shadow as it passes along the sea shore or mountain trail or sidewalk or deck of a cruise ship. Focus on the joy you feel when sharing your experience with a loved one. The more real you can make the experience in your mind the more the Universe will have more to build upon and manifest.

Make it as real as you possibly can. Do you want an exotic vacation? Then create the scene looking out of your hotel window on to the lush landscape of your Five Star Resort. Create the scene looking back the other way at your hotel. Pick out your room; the one with the great view and wide balcony. Create the scene as you travel to your destination. Create the

> Be thankful for what you have; you'll end up having more. If you concentrate on what you don't have, you will never, ever have enough.—Oprah Winfrey

smell and taste of the exceptional food you will eat. See yourself and your loved one relaxing on a chartered yacht in the sunny Aegean Sea. Create the feeling of happiness, contentment and well-being you have when you are on vacation.

Take a hint from Julia Cameron's exceptional book, *The Artist's Way*. Start and maintain a daily Gratitude/Abundance Journal. Every night before you retire, take five minutes and record those things which manifested in your life that day and be thankful for them. Did you take a walk and notice the birds or vegetation? Did someone pay you a compliment? Were you particularly inspired by something a friend said? Are your children doing well, even a little bit? Be grateful and record the positive feelings in your life for that day. Then write "Thank You God for my blessings today." Even if nothing seemed to go your way, you can write "Thank You God for a new day tomorrow."

Many people find their way to prosperity blocked by feelings of unworthiness. These feelings, programmed in at an early age, form a barrier that many find difficult to overcome.

We will go further into the concept of affirmations later in this book, but for now here is a brief look.

Allow me to affirm for you here and now: *You are worthy of your desires.*

Repeat after me using the Biblical I AM name of God for emphasis: "I AM worthy of my desires."

And again: "I AM worthy of my desires."

And finally, "I AM worthy of my desires."

Rebuild that negative self-talk into positive images using the affirmation and denial technique. Affirmations are simple, direct statements of Truth as it applies to your desires. Affirm "I am worthy of God's love" and "God gave me an assignment and I am going to complete it with more resources than I see now."

At first, it may seem to you that you are only mouthing the words. But after 21 days of saying your affirmations, your subconscious begins to believe them as real. If you find yourself slipping (and who doesn't) just reaffirm your affirmation.

In addition to affirmations, you also have the tool of denials as one of your spiritual tools.

Denials are statements which cancel out negative influences. Simply put, if you find that you are giving away your energy to another person or situation, you may wish to invoke some denial statements. Deny "That person's opinion of me has no power over my life. I deny it the power it seeks from me." Use the Golden Rule (which by the way is in all religious traditions in one form or another) by loving yourself and others the way you wish to be loved. This simple thought will increase your feelings of worthiness and clear the way for your on-coming Abundance.

Act as if you have already received your desire.

Feel the excitement when setting out on your journey. Speak as if you have received your tickets. Think of it as a Done Deal. Affirm "As I see it, so it is." Express your gratitude for what you desire having become manifest.

If you desire a new car, feel the satisfaction of driving around in a brand new vehicle. Smell the new car smell. Think about all the great places you can go. Feel the wind on your face, the sunlight glinting, and the quiet sound of the engine.

If you want a relationship, hold the feeling of love in your heart. Build an image of your ideal mate. Put that list where you can see it several times a day. See your mate standing next to you as you read the list together. Mentally have a mirror in your mind. This mirror reflects a happy and prosperous image of you. Also in that reflection is an image of your perfect mate. The face may be obscured, but you can see their hair and body type and feel the love emanating from their heart.

Here is a technique my friend Jimmy used to help him uncover some of the aspects of his perfect mate that he may have previously overlooked: On-Line Dating. Dating services have a great application: the profile builder. Many times you can access these without charge. He used the profile to first build his own *honest* profile. I emphasize honest because this book is all about breaking out of the artificial shells we have built and establishing the true you. Jimmy used a

> Desire is the starting point of all achievement, not a hope, not a wish, but a keen pulsating desire, which transcends everything. When your desires are strong enough you will appear to possess superhuman powers to achieve.
> –Napoleon Hill

recent picture, even though his hair color and waist size may have been different from his ideals. (He could always change them later by using some of the techniques in this book.)

After he built and printed off his honest profile, he submitted it for evaluation. The sites will make an evaluation of the kind of person who may be interested in his background, gender, experiences and leisure activities. He used that document to build his ideal relationship, even though he didn't plan on using the dating site past the trial period. (Later, Jimmy did send them a tithe in appreciation for the insights he gained.)

Then he visualized himself going on enjoyable dates and outings with his ideal mate. Jimmy thought about places he could go and things that they could see together. Remember, he was establishing a relationship with Abundance.

How did Jimmy's exercise for a new relationship work out? He had known someone in his church for several years, and one day something clicked in his mind and he asked her out. He is now happily in a long-term committed relationship with his perfect mate, and he gives this process all the credit.

If you want an improved work environment, visualize harmony and ease in the office. Know that tension, conflict and disagreement will only affect you if you allow it to.

By simply acting as if you have already received your desire, you activate the Law of Attraction to bring it to you. Always express gratitude to Source for your visions.

Take Action, or as the Quakers say "When you pray, move your feet."

Let's say you want the vacation of a lifetime. Stop by a travel agent and pick up some brochures. Ask the agent about exotic destinations.

If you are in a place where it isn't convenient to go to an agent, then go on line and look at images of your destination. Check out what side trips you can take. Pick out the clothing you are taking. Look up a house-, pet- or plant-sitter to watch after your home while you are away. Make plans to hold your mail for the duration. Make your image tangible any way you can. Most importantly, continue saying thank you to God/Source/the Universe as if you have already received your trip.

If you want a new vehicle, go to the dealership and test drive the car of your dreams. Imprint the feel of the road and the new smell. Look at the options and make up a list of what you want in your brand new car.

If you want a new relationship, go to some of the places you will enjoy together: a concert, museum, tractor pull, whatever. You are letting Source know that you are open and receptive to the Abundance the Universe has in store for you.

But don't be impatient.

Let Go and Let God.

As hard as it may seem, now is the time to detach yourself from the outcome. Allow the Universe, in its perfection, to provide your manifested desire. Letting go and letting God simply means that you are not going to be the gardener who pulls up his plants every few days to see if they have grown any more. That doesn't work for the plants and it won't work for your creation efforts.

How important is detachment from outcome? It's important enough that for every month since it was founded in 1924, the inspirational publication *The Daily Word* has devoted a day to it. Pick up any copy of the publication from any month of any year, look at the index, and you will find a daily devotional for *Let Go and Let God*.

The concept of letting go of the outcome is central to many precepts as well as 12-Step programs. If you want the Universe to provide you with abundance, don't stand in the middle of the floor and cry "Where is it? I've been waiting two whole days! I want my

Abundance and I want it now!" If someone demanded something from you in that way, how eager would you be to go to work?

There is another way to ask. Inspirational writer Mary Kupferle notes, "Take time to be quiet, to be still and contemplate the Truth that God's love is right there with you, that God's light is now shining throughout your mind to reveal what you need to see and know. Listen within and let God's wisdom gently turn your thoughts over and over until the questions become answers, the doubts become newborn faith. You will see that everything has been and is working for your good." **When you mentally release your ego from the situation, limitations disappear, and God's light ignites your way to Abundance.**

If you can't trust God to give you what you desire, who are you going to trust? You may know people who have trusted the Stock Market, and how well has that worked out for them in terms of personal happiness? Consider some of the great financial institutions who have lost billions of dollars in bad investments due to economic conditions.

Give Thanks.

Gratitude is the WD-40 that makes the Law of Attraction work. Gratitude for the simplest events or feelings allows Spirit to move in and through your life ever more freely. As the 14th Century mystic Meister Eckhart said "The most powerful prayer you can ever say is 'Thank You'."

I was once complimented on a sweater I was wearing. I began my usual "Oh, this old thing? I've had it for ages. In fact…" I was cut off by my friend Carter. He said "Alan, the proper response is simply 'Thank You'." In that moment, I learned to receive gratitude as well as to express it.

As renowned author and publisher Louise L. Hay, stated in an on-line newsletter: "Gratitude brings more to be grateful about. It increases your abundant life. Lack of gratitude or complaining, brings little to rejoice about. Complainers always find that they have little good in their life, or they don't enjoy what they *do* have.

"The Universe always gives us what we believe we deserve.

"For quite a while now, I've been accepting every compliment and every present with: 'I accept with joy and pleasure and gratitude.' I've learned that the Universe loves this expression, and I constantly get the most wonderful presents!"

I am reminded of the story of the family sitting down to dinner. Mom, Dad and Sonny were dining on one of Mom's specialties: Sauerkraut Soufflé. Several times throughout the meal, Sonny said "Thanks Mom. What a meal!"

Now Mom knew that Sonny was not a fan of the dish she had served. Finally she said "What's wrong with you? You never used to like this." Sonny said "The teacher said we should be thankful for everything today. And I am!" He continued under his breath, "But I still hate it."

Actor Henry Fonda said "I cry at a good steak," meaning he was overwhelmed by the gratitude he felt that went into the entire meal.

When I finish a meal, I always give it a quiet round of applause. It is my way of giving thanks for everything that went into it, especially if I prepared it myself. (And I'm a great cook, even if I do say so.)

A little gratitude goes a long way. Use it often to enhance your Abundance.

Get ready to receive.

A sense of anticipation of your good is an essential part of the Prosperity Code. Nature and yappy little dogs abhor a vacuum. Create a vacuum in the area you desire so the Universe can rush in and fill it. If you desire a new wardrobe, for example, simply clean out your closet. Pass your clothing along to an organization or individual that will put them to good use.

> If you want greater prosperity in your life, start forming a vacuum to receive it. —Catherine Ponder

Let's say that you want a new or updated

wardrobe. Make a bee-line to the closet and pick half of what's hanging there to give away. That's right: Give it away.

Take your clothing, shoes, accessories and other items to either the Salvation Army or Goodwill Industries. You will be providing other people with the opportunity to use your gifts. You will be tithing to them so they can accomplish what it is for them to accomplish. Pay it forward.

Back to your now spacious closet, put pictures of what kinds of clothing you would like to be hanging there. Imagine your feelings when you can take your pick of nice new (to you) clothing.

You are now ready to receive your new wardrobe.

If you want a new car, go clean out the garage so you will have space to park it. Determine the resale price of your old car through any of a number of on-line services to get an idea of its trade-in value. Or you can write up the classified ad to sell it when your new car arrives. If the car is on its last legs, then plan to donate it to your local NPR or PBS station so they can benefit. Finally, plan a celebratory day trip to embark upon in your brand new car the first chance you get.

You are now ready to receive your new car.

Continue this process for whatever it is that you desire. Make room for it and the Universe will provide.

You have joined a partnership for manifesting Abundance. You are partners with Spirit/ God/ the Universe in collaboration to materialize your desires. God is the best partner you can ever have. His guidance about financial affairs will lead you straight to Abundance. Leave the concerns and worries to your Senior Partner. Leave the hard decisions and difficult situations to His management. His style is beneficial to all concerned. He authored the original win/ win concept.

There is a famous Scriptural passage wherein God actually asks to be tested. It is the only place in the Bible where He does this.

In Malachi 3:10 (KJV) it is written "Prove me now herewith, saith Jehovah of hosts, if I will not open you the windows of heaven and pour out a blessing that there shall not be room enough to receive it."

So, has your way worked so far in your life? Go ahead and give God's way a try. And hang on!

You have nothing to lose except fear, pain, lack, depression and ill health.

Key Number 5:
Faith-You Must Believe

F amed movie producer Mike Todd, who produced the classic 1957 *Around the World in 80 Days*, once said, "I have often been broke, but I have never been poor." He said that because he believed in his innate entitlement to prosperity.

When you believe that prosperity is your birthright, your destiny, your purpose here in this life, you will be well on your way to cracking the code. You will be where millions of truly prosperous people are today.

Why? Because it is not "The World" that makes you poor!

It is not "Them, out there" who stand between you and a life of abundance and prosperous ease. It is not a certain someone or "someones" who are standing between you and your 45 day trip around the world on the Queen Mary II.

> If you think that everything is someone else's fault, you will suffer a lot. –The Dalai Lama

It is *you*. Or more specifically, it is what is between your ears.

"Me?" you say. "How can I be at fault when society or family or poor choices have done all this damage to me and my finances?"

It is not the world that affects you.

It is your decision how you *allow it to* get to you.

Marie, a student in one of my prosperity classes, reported one week that she had been told of a transmission leak in her car. "Normally, I would have become upset and frustrated about this," she reported. "But thanks to the class, I have learned that everything in life is a choice. I can choose to be upset or not. This time, I chose not to let it upset me. I can't tell you how much better I feel."

Now that you're totally confused, let me explain.

One of the hardest concepts to get your arms around is the concept of taking responsibility for your life. It has been said that a slight or insult will hurt only if you let it. Someone will make you angry or upset only if you let them. Life will make you upset if you let it.

Where did you learn to be upset at life? Who told you that you are not good enough, not important enough, not attractive enough, not artistic or coordinated enough? Where did you learn your set of limiting beliefs?

It almost always happens in the growing-up process we call "socialization." During that complex, long-term process, children go from being the best singers, best dancers, fastest runners, outstanding artists, champion kickball players to being discouraged and molded into other people's (i.e.: society's) concepts of how they should behave.

> The success of our economy has always depended not just on the size of our gross domestic product, but on the reach of our prosperity, on the ability to extend opportunity to every willing heart -- not out of charity, but because it is the surest route to our common good. –Barack Obama, 2009

Robert Fulghum, the author of *All I Need to Know, I Learned in Kindergarten*, tells of going into pre-schools around the country and asking the kids "Who is a good painter?" Everyone raised their hands and gleefully got ready to paint. Then he asked "Who is a good singer?" and he was greeted by a chorus of voices singing their own praises as the world's best singers.

He also asked the children about running, skipping rope, building with blocks, and was assured that every one of those skills were abundantly present in his audiences.

Then he asked the same questions of college students. One or two in a group would meekly acknowledge that they *might* have a little artistic talent, but only if they were art or music majors or art majors, or physical education majors.

Maybe you've seen a two-year-old on a rampage shouting the only word they've heard over and over: "No!" Right after "Mama" and "Papa", the child hears "No" the most. Now, we say we do it to protect the child, and that is certainly one factor. But "No" is often heard in other contexts as well.

Right now, that dreaded *no* word is sitting deeply buried in your mind. It sits up and barks at you many times a day. The next time you hear it: ask yourself whose voice is it? Is it a parent's voice? A sibling's? A friend's? An enemy's? Or, was it the second grade teacher who told you in front of the whole class that you'd never be any good at anything?

And what the heck did they know?

Those voices were only repeating what older voices told them. An ugly mindset of lack and limitation comes cascading down the generations to squat its obnoxious self deeply in your mind, holding you back from your birthright of abundance and plenty.

And you generally have no idea that it is there.

So how do you move it out? How do you overcome generations of programming which got you where you are now?

The Christian Bible did not spring fully formed as the King James Version all at once. It went through many translations and editors before it even got to that stage. There are more than 50 major translations of the Bible in existence today. But the language the first texts were written in was Aramaic, the language spoken by Jesus. The original Aramaic translation of "Ask, and it shall be given to you", (Matthew 7:7, KJV) is "Ask without hidden motive, and be surrounded by your answer."

So when you ask, and see it done in your mind's eye, you will be surrounded by your answer and astonished by your power.

By the way, Marie found there was nothing wrong with her transmission.

Recognize those inner voices for what they are. Recognize that they have no basis in reality. Those voices don't know what they're talking about.

Review: You can use two very practical tools to do this: Affirmations and Denials.

Affirmations are sayings you repeat again and again to overcome your inner nonsense. The affirmation can be as simple as repeating "I am prosperous."

Over a very short period, you will begin to feel the energy the affirmation brings to you. Prosperity teacher Stretton Smith states if you say "I am prosperous" with feeling and belief, at least 100 times in the morning and 100 times before going to bed, for 45 days, you will have established a new habit and undone a lifetime of damage. By the time you have passed your tenth day of doing this little exercise, you will begin to feel the power of your words sinking into your mind and heart. Smith suggests that positive affirmations such as: "The prospering power of God *within me* prospers me now," puts the cause of your prosperity well within you and your belief that you can do this with a little help from a Friend. You may also like: "The Source of All *within me* manifests my prosperity now."

Jesus, that long-ago millionaire from Nazarus, famously advised his followers to seek first the kingdom within and, he promised, everything else would be added to it. Based on that simple statement, you know where you base your affirmations.

The power of affirmations manifest themselves in direct proportion to the energy you put into them.

There is a more extensive list of suggested affirmations at the end of this chapter.

Denials are used to negate the power a situation has over you and your life. If someone is making you angry, an example of a denial statement is: "I refuse to give this person any of my power." What are you giving your power away to? It's like saying: "I'm sick. *You* go to the hospital." You're giving your power to the *effect* of the situation, not to the *cause*.

You may want to use the denial: "My health problems have no power over my life." Or "My income is not dependent on the economy." Or work with "My family's negative attitudes have no effect on me." Many seemingly miraculous healings have been observed through the power of denials. They work best in tandem with affirmations.

Myrtle Fillmore, the co-founder of the Unity movement, used affirmations and denials to heal herself of TB in the 1880s. She sat alone in a room and spoke to the cells of her body, telling them that God didn't make junk, and they were going to be in perfect health. Her dedicated devotion to the process of affirmations and denials helped start a prayer-based nonsectarian movement that now is all over the world.

She used a combination of affirmations ("All my cells are healthy") and denials ("Disease has no power over my life") . In doing so, she recognized the power of prayer.

We all pray.

All day.

We pray 24/7.

We don't necessarily get down on our knees, clasp our hands and look skyward.

Every second of our life contains a prayer and a prophecy. Usually, it's a prayer that goes something like this: "I'm going to be late. They're not going to like me. The cleaner is going to ruin my best sweater. The dog is going to mess in the house again, probably on the oriental carpet. My boss hates me. My paycheck is puny. I'll never make enough money..." and so on *ad nauseum*. These prayers, running in the background, are every bit as powerful as a conscious prayer. They are heard by the Great Copy Machine that is the Universe and become fulfilled as prophecy.

In fact, we can make ourselves sick with our prayers.

Or, we can make ourselves well.

To do this, we can consciously pray, "My presentation is going to go great today. I'm going to hit the green light at every intersection, my day will go smoothly, the kids will have a good report card", etc. We can easily feed the Great Universe Copy Shop with positive intentions and statements when we consciously remember what we are praying.

It's your choice.

So, which are you going to choose? Remember, it was your best thinking that got you to where you are today, as many of the12-Step programs remind us.

Are you going to change your thinking so you can change your life?

Can you commit to that?

Breaking habits is a tough job. Studies have shown that it takes a minimum of 21 days of practice to establish a new habit, although Stretton Smith recommends 45 days. Take one affirmation such as "I am worthy of all the Universe has for me!" and repeat it 100 times upon arising (the shower is a good place for this) and 100 times before retiring for 21 days.

Another hint: By simply changing "I *can't* afford this" to "How *can I* afford this?" you cut through the lack and open the way for the Universe to figure out how you will achieve your desires. See your monthly bills not as obligations but as blessings. Indeed, they will bless those to whom you send them. The people at the power company or the water works put their energy into providing you with electricity and water. They deserve their blessings from you and their other customers.

Abundance may not seek you out if you have a job you hate. But Abundance will find you no matter where you are if you elevate your consciousness from lack to plenty *even if the physical aspect has not yet materialized*.

My friend Nancy Ennis often tells the old story that involves an unhappily married man going to see his psychiatrist. "Doc," he pleaded, "you've got to help me! My wife has let herself go, she doesn't work, she won't keep the house clean and the kids are running wild. I need a sure fire way to get out of this mess and teach her a lesson."

The Doctor considered for a moment, and then said: "I have it! Here's what you need to do: On your way home from my office, stop and get her a bouquet of red roses, or her favorite flowers. Then tell her you would like to take her to dinner at a great restaurant. While you're dining, tell her that you would like her to go out with her girlfriends once a week and that you will watch the kids. Pay her compliments on her hair, makeup and fashions. Then after 4 weeks of that, walk out and leave her! I guarantee that she will be shocked and will never bother you again."

Some time passed and it was more than six months before the Doctor ran into the man at a diner.

"Tell me," said the Doc, "What happed with your marriage? Did you leave your wife?"

The man looked shocked. "Are you kidding?" he asked incredulously. "I went and took your advice, bringing her flowers, paying her compliments, giving her some free time and so on. And do you know, we fell in love again! I wouldn't leave her for anything in the world!"

Simply by changing his mind and altering his behavior, this man was able to bring an Abundance of love into his relationship.

Although he did not use Affirmations as such, he made his behavior affirm what he wished.

Use Affirmations.

You can make up your own affirmations. Remember to use the powerful I AM statement whenever possible. It is also useful to claim your good NOW, not tomorrow or next month.

As discussed earlier, **Affirmations are positive statements and thoughts we can use to reprogram the negative feelings we have about abundance.** You may wish to start by using some of the affirmations listed below.

I am open and receptive to God's living truth as It manifests my Abundance, now.

God is my partner; in Him I have perfect trust and faith for our mutual good, now.

I am ready, willing and 100% able to manifest my prosperity now.

Regardless of the so-called economy, my financial health is richly increased through the action of God.

Every day in every way I am becoming more and more prosperous.

I love my life! I am grateful for the life I am leading now.

As I view the world today, I see and act on rich opportunities to increase my prosperity.

I am now open, receptive, responsive and obedient to the Living Spirit of Truth.

I am thankful that the Divine now provides me with all the answers I need, regardless of the situation.

I am grateful that every one of my bills has turned into a blessing. I now release these blessings freely and with love.

As I go through my day, I will shower those around me with positive thoughts and the Universe will return this positive energy to me a hundred times over.

My good does not come from the physical world but instead manifests through the energy and love of God.

I am always open to receive God's guidance in all aspects of my life.

When I am still, I hear God's abundant thoughts for me and I am motivated to act upon them.

> It is because of their tranquil thoughts / That creatures go to prosperity.
> —Buddha

I am receiving all the good God has for me now. I am perpetually prosperous.

I am richly and truly blessed now.

God has given me all power for my highest good in my body, mind and spirit. I claim that power and experience it now.

I accept and claim the divine resolution in this situation now.

I give so that I may receive my blessings back from the Universe blessed and multiplied.

I am worthy. I deserve all the good I receive from a beneficent Universe.

I now ask for divine guidance and thereby receive new gifts from my Source of all good.

I am open to positive new outcomes in my life, world and affairs now.

The universe provides more than I need to succeed now.

Money now flows to me easily and continually without effort on my part.

All gifts of money, favors, and donations I give come back to me and blessed and multiplied.

Every day and in every way, I am completely worthy of all Abundance the Universe gives me now.

I have a mustard seed and I'm not afraid to use it.

Key Number 6:
Give, Give, Give

S poiler Alert: This may the hardest part of your journey, depending on your previous experience. What we will discuss here can be very daunting for those not accustomed to increasing their prosperity. The first piece of this is the biggest and hardest for most people to get their arms around. This is a vital part of the Prosperity Code: your commitment to the Universe to give back to it.

It's called **tithing**.

Go ahead and say it: "Tithing". And try not to look like you're eating a lemon.

See, that didn't hurt, did it?

There is a reason why the ancient Israelites had a society based on tithing: It worked. It worked for all members of society. **When one gives back a mere 10% of one's bounty, the returns are immense.**

We are, by nature, a generous species. Watch what happens when you see an infant or very young child. They instinctively reach out and want to share. They have not learned the behavior of withholding and refusing to give. They are still part of the oneness of the universe and know without a doubt that there is more than enough for everyone.

Stories of the effectiveness of tithing abound.

The founder of a major restaurant chain made a commitment to tithing before he opened his first location. His chain grew and flourished even in places where others had failed. He kept his commitment to the Universe and kept tithing. In fact, he increased his tithe to 20% much to the horror of his CFO. But his business continued to develop and expand even more!

One of my prosperity teachers told me of a farmer who decided to try tithing as an experiment on his faltering family-owned farm. He reluctantly agreed to set aside 10% of his grain sales and donate the money to various charities. That first year, he broke even and was wishing that he hadn't given his donations away. But he discovered that the farms around his had suffered substantial losses and he, by comparison, was well off. The second year started out poorly for all the farmers in the area who were beset by floods and storms. Yet at the end of the season, the farmer found that he had 20% more money than the year before. And the quality of his grain was superior. So he happily tithed 10 % of his harvest again.

At the end of five years, the farmer found it necessary to hire more hands and rent out more land from his amazed neighbors so his thriving farm could keep up with the demand for his superior quality grain. Eventually, he was able to send his children to college without resorting to any loans. He and his family learned a valuable lesson about the awesome power of tithing.

Jill discovers the power of tithing.

In one of my prosperity classes, Jill was especially resistant to the concept of tithing. As a teacher in a school system which was readjusting its personnel on a constant basis, she was afraid that she would not have a job and therefore would not have any money to live on. During the class, we worked on the concept "Your job is not your source; God is your Source."

Eventually, she grudgingly agreed to tithe.

We didn't see her the next week, and I wondered if she had given up.

A week later, Jill was back in class. During our check-in I noticed that she was very excited, so I called on her first.

"I wasn't here last week," she reported, "because some friends and I went to New York. On the way, we stopped off in Jersey City to gamble. I didn't have much money, so I sat at the penny slot machines while I waited for the others to come back from their blackjack tables. I had a few cents in my pocket, so I fed the machine." She smiled a big, bright smile. "And do you know, I won a jackpot!" We all cheered for her.

"But wait!" She held up her hands. "I won two more jackpots! Now *that's* what I call the power of the tithe!" Jill has happily and consistently tithed since then.

How I became a tither.

My own experience with tithing started when I had the first opportunity to hear master prosperity teacher Edwene Gaines. I was going through a particularly rocky part of life and was afraid I wouldn't have enough money to pay the relatively modest rent on a studio apartment. My industry consulting business had recently lost its major client and I had no idea where my next contract was going to come from.

Edwene, in her charming Southern/Texas twang, went into great detail about how effective tithing is. She made the point that tithing helps you develop a greater sense of abundance. By giving 10% of your income, you're programming your subconscious to believe in abundance thinking. This can make you more open and receptive to receiving money. If you think abundance, she said, you will experience abundance. "Pay God first," she said, "And He will return the compliment."

I figured that I had nothing to lose, so I opened my checkbook. I had $87.50 as a very carefully calculated balance. When it came time to collect the offering, I dutifully wrote out a check for $8.75 and put it in the collection plate.

The next day, the phone rang with a proposal to co-author my first book. Many other lucrative opportunities followed. And I have never looked back. In fact, my tithe last year came out at 12% of my income.

Tithing FAQs.

Here are some frequently asked questions about the practice of tithing:

Do I tithe on the gross or the net?

If you are going to be faithful to the Prosperity Code's concept of tithing, give on the gross. In fact, I know of people who have given a tithe based on a loan or mortgage they received. In the case of the mortgage, they were surprised to find that they had paid the note off within 2 years without breaking a sweat.

Do I always have to tithe to a charity?

According to the Prosperity Code, you give your tithe to whatever source *spiritually nourishes* you. If an individual, such as a waitress or cabbie, says something in passing that allows you to realize a deep spiritual insight, then give them a tithe (not only a tip) and acknowledge that they helped you out. There's nothing wrong with giving to charity as long as you have first tithed to what nourishes you spiritually, whether it is a place of worship or accidental philosopher.

Do I have to tithe a full 10%?

The Law of Giving and Receiving states you get back what you give. If you want to give less than 10%, then you will receive that much less back from the Universe. **I challenge you to tithe for 30 days.** I guarantee that by the end of that trial period, you will be fully convinced of its power.

Take the case of Cathy and Don. They had recently relocated and both were having challenges finding the right work for their respective talents. They acknowledged resistance to the concept of tithing, but eventually agreed to give it a try. They started tithing a small amount. Almost immediately, Cathy's home-based business experienced a major influx of orders. Don found not one, but two jobs that would allow him to use his previous experience and training. They are now enthusiastic supporters of tithing a full 10% because they experienced its power.

Is it greedy to desire material goods?

Being rich does not equate to being greedy according to the Prosperity Code. The Aramaic translation of the often misquoted statement "Money is the root of all evil" saying from the King James Bible is more correctly translated as *"Avarice is the source of all malevolence."* To open yourself to all the riches the Universe has in store for you is not being greedy; it is accepting your birthright as the prosperous child of God. Besides, as a child of God, you love to share and when you share, there is no room for greed in your life.

Isn't tithing a big pyramid scheme?

Where the heck did *that* come from?

Giving opens the way for receiving. In order to create activity in finances, one should give. Tithing or giving one-tenth of one's income, is an old Jewish custom, and is sure to bring increase. Many of the richest men in this country have been tithers, and I have never known it to fail as an investment. The tenth-part goes forth and returns blessed and multiplied. But the gift or tithe must be given with love and cheerfulness, for 'God loveth a cheerful giver.' Bills should be paid cheerfully, all money should be sent forth fearlessly and with a blessing. –Florence Scovel Shinn

You are the one who benefits by giving to and receiving from the Universe. You're not putting your money into Mr. Ponzi's scheme. You are putting your prosperity energy into a universal multiplier which will return the energy to you increased and multiplied many times over.

Isn't money filthy?

Nowhere in the Bible does it say that God loves poverty or illness or disabilities. True, over the years, some have decided to give up material goods in an effort to cleanse themselves from so-called earthly desires. They may be the ones who talked about "filthy lucre," or "ill-gotten gains," the misquoted "Money is the root of all evil," or other negative connotations on money. Money is only a symbol of energy. That piece of printed paper or metal with a design on it merely represents the ability to acquire something of equal value.

Why 10%? Why not 5 % or 13%?

The Hebrew mystics assigned symbolic values to numbers. The number 10 stands for increase because every time you pass it, you are entering a new cycle of numbers. When you pass the number 10, you get increase. Thus when you add 1 to 10+9 (19), you get 10+10 (20) and so on. You have entered a new cycle when you go past 10 and its multiples.

Why can it be so difficult to tithe?

When people are raised in a consciousness of greed or selfishness and fear, it is very difficult to overcome the programming of taking and replace it with giving. They are afraid of letting their "hard-earned money" go to be replaced by "Easy Abundance" as brought forth by tithing.

There is the story of two bills: a $100 bill and a $1.00 bill, both printed on the same day at the Bureau of Printing and Engraving in Washington. They agreed to stay in touch during their lives. Several years later, they meet in the same cash drawer.

The shabby and worn dollar bill spoke up first: "Hey, C Note, what's going on? Where have you been all these years?"

The crisp, dapper $100 bill, looking fresh and relaxed answered "Oh, you know, the usual. Only the finest places: restaurants, spas, cruises, Wall Street, the jet set. I had lots of great experiences and have been around the world three times. How about you, Bill?"

The slightly ragged dollar bill looked down dejectedly and sighed: "You know, the usual: church plate, church plate, church plate!"

Make friends with money. As we will discuss in the chapter on core values, money, in and of itself, has no power over you. It can do a lot for you if you let it. It can also ruin your life if you let it. Remember that holding on to your money does not bring any more to you. Like love, you have to give some away to get some back.

A recent Harvard University study concluded that indeed money *can* buy happiness, if it is spent correctly, as reported on in TED 2011.

Using representative populations from all over the world, researchers gave one group some money and told them to spend it on themselves. They gave the second group some money and told them to spend it on someone else, but not on themselves. They measured the groups' respective levels of happiness before and after spending their money.

The group which was told to spend the money on themselves reported little or no change in their levels of happiness.

However, the group who was told to spend their money on someone else reported markedly higher levels of happiness. They also reported a greater awareness of themselves as a team.

The results were the same regardless of the amount of money the respective groups received. So we see that your potential for happiness increases when you spend some money on someone else, especially if that someone nourishes you spiritually.

Other Forms of Tithing

Two other forms of giving include tithing your Time and Talents.

Tithe of your time.

Are you always running out of time? Are you consistently late for appointments? Are you always in a panic to complete a task?

If you want more time, give some of it away. Tithe your time to your source of spiritual nourishment. If your church needs volunteers (and I don't know of a church who doesn't) call the office and find out where you could help out. The office always needs papers filed or folded; the grounds could always use a clean-up, the interior might need a coat of paint. **Give of your time and you will find you have more time to do other things.**

Tithe your talents.

If you want to expand your talents, tithe on your talents. If you can read out loud, volunteer with the local school to be a reader in elementary school once a week. If you can stir a pot, go to a local soup kitchen and volunteer. Our Homeless Neighbors can always use more willing hands and talents to help solve it. Call your local Food Bank and volunteer to sort cans or pick up donations. Finally, three words: "Meals on Wheels." Bring some light, love and substance to those who can no longer leave their homes.

> Quality is more important than quantity. The universe amplifies thought into circumstance. Begin giving and let God perfect your giving. —Brad Jensen.

Giving also extends to love. If you are feeling particularly unloved, then go out and give someone you know a big socially appropriate hug. After doing this several times, you will feel the warmth of love in your heart. You will feel loved because you gave some love to others.

Give your appreciation to others as well, and you will receive appreciation back. Appreciate your family, friends, co-workers, neighbors, fellow commuters. Appreciate your food, your pets, your home, your transportation and life. **Appreciate as a habit.**

Instead of saying "Oh God, *another* day," say instead "Oh God! Another Day!" Appreciation will enable you to notice things you may have missed previously, or forgotten.

As you are giving of your time and talents, you will meet and interact with people who will, in turn, give you energy and ideas for your Abundance.

You may be the only Bible other people read. As you give, so you receive in all aspects of your life.

As you continue to unlock the Prosperity Code, you will find that giving is a fundamental key to your success.

Key Number 7:
The Secret Missing Link

A s noted earlier, there are a many books and programs on the market purporting to increase their readers' abundance and prosperity. For the most part they follow similar formats. But, a very few have what I am calling the Missing Secret Link: Alignment with your life's purpose.

Will the desire you are working toward work *with* or *against* your life's purpose?

And, what, exactly is your life's purpose? Why did you come here? What is the goal you set for yourself?

To get to the answer, we need to step into the weird here for a moment.

A quick review of the literature on Near Death Experiences (NDEs) often shows people reporting they came into this life with a set of goals. The goals could be as complex as

> All programming for prosperity should be built on spiritual foundations. The first step is to enter the spiritual dimension, the alpha level, and determine what your purpose in life is. Find out what you are here for, what you are supposed to do with your life.
> —José Silva

finding a major medical breakthrough, overcoming addiction(s) or parenting a child with special needs. Or even being an individual with special needs.

The body of work by psychologist Michael Newton, Ph.D. or popular psychic Sylvia Browne shows a consistent pattern with respondent after respondent. Basically, after a soul leaves this earthly phase of life, it has a chance to review how well it has accomplished the goals it came into the body to accomplish.

On a soul level, it's really no more complicated than going to the grocery store for eggs and milk. When you get back from the store, you ask "Did I get the eggs and milk I went for?" If you did, great! You can put something else on your To-Do List. If you forgot what you went to the store to get (and most of us do), then you put it on the list for the next time you go to the store.

As souls, we forget why we went to the proverbial store because we have amnesia. We have that loss of memory so we can't cheat and go directly to Go and collect the $200 without going around the board once. **We have to actually work to reach our goals.**

When we decide it is time to come back to the physical phase of life, we review our list and try to impress waypoints which might trigger an impulse to follow-up. The feeling of heightened awareness in certain situations, such as when you met your mate, can be attributed to this impression process.

This section of the book will endeavor to help you determine what your life purpose is.

Time for an Exercise!

Find a sheet of paper and on it make two columns. Label the first column "Things I Like To Do" and the second column "Things I Don't Like to Do."

Review your experiences in life and write down the things that make your heart sing. It could be as simple as working on a hobby or as complex as solving higher mathematical problems. What activity causes your subjective time to pass in a flash? What activity literally swallows you up and you love? What constitutes bliss for you? Don't worry if nothing comes to mind. We'll have an exercise later to help break things loose. Then you can repeat this exercise.

Now move to the column of things you don't like. What activities cause the time to slow to a snail's pace? What is it that you do that makes getting up in the morning difficult? Note that most people do not have as much of a problem with this column as with the other. Use additional paper if you need it. And you probably will.

If your Do Not Like list includes your job, then possibly your job is not a part of your life purpose. It could be supporting you, but at what cost to you?

Now, take a look at your "I Like" list. What stands out? Perhaps you have discovered that you love to garden, or draw or even work those math problems.

These Likes are clues to your life's purpose. If you like to garden, it may be that your life purpose is to provide organic herbs, fruits vegetables or flowers to beautify and enhance the environment. If you're drawn to drawing, you may have a purpose in design or illustration. If you like math, you may have a software company or even an auditing job in your future.

> What I know is, is that if you do work that you love, and the work fulfills you, the rest will come.— Oprah Winfrey

Look at your "I Don't Like" list. If you have some desires that run along the same lines as things you don't like, ask yourself "Why do I want this particular desire?" If the answer you get back is "Because someone expects me to do it," or "I am doing it to prove someone else wrong," you may wish to review your desires list.

Another Exercise.

Now, ask yourself the following questions and write the answers down. Write the answers in 30 seconds or less. And be honest, since you are the only one who will see this. Don't edit, just write.

Who inspires you most?

Which qualities inspire you?

Is this person a close friend or family member?

A movie star or athlete?

A statesman or religious leader?

Write down the qualities of each person who inspires you.

What activities make you lose track of time?

Are you a gardener who waters the soil with your sweat?

Do you like to take out a sketch pad and draw or paint?

Do you get lost in your stamp or coin collection or another hobby?

What activities make you ask: "Where did the time go?"

What makes you smile, giggle or laugh?

Do you enjoy watching children frolicking at the playground or animals at the zoo?

Do you get a kick out of Garfield or a cartoon in *The New Yorker*?

Do you enjoy puns, pratfalls or a situation comedy on television?

What brings a smile to your face and warmth to your heart?

If you were asked to teach something, what would it be? This does not necessarily mean standing in front of a classroom of children and teaching reading, although it could. We are all teachers in one way or another. What would you teach? Would you like to take youngsters on a nature trail and point out the flora and fauna? Could you teach music or art appreciation in a community or senior center?

What makes you feel good about yourself?

There is something you can do that very few other people can do.

What is it?

Can you bake a sinfully delicious German Chocolate Cake to bring to family gatherings? A cake that is so popular that it's gone before you can have any?

Can you transform your yard into a neighborhood showplace with ease?

In what subject do people typically ask you for help?

In what area of your life are you the *Go-To* person?

Are you a gifted computer tech?

Do you have a natural ability to visualize the best use of a space?

Do you have the magic touch in fixing appliances or small engines?

In what area do people call you the "Guru"?

Have you made a Bucket List? If not, put together a small list of ten things you want to do before you depart this planet.

What skills, abilities or gifts have you developed thus far in your life?

Do you love to write poetry? (Aside: check with some of the greeting card companies.)

Can you nurse an ailing animal back to full health?

Are you a gifted painter, sculptor or card reader?

When you see a situation, do you naturally see a solution to any problem?

Can you speak in front of a crowd (despite the fact that many people are more afraid of public speaking than they are of dying)?

What floats your boat?

Given your talents, passions and values, how would you use your abilities to serve, to help, to contribute to the planet, to society and to your family?

Where would you, as a unique expression of God, be of the most service?

How can you take the talents you have developed over years and mesh them with others' talents for the good of all?

The point of this exercise is to allow you to discover if your desires are congruent with, or at cross purposes to your life purpose. If you are studying for relatively isolated life of an IT tech because that is where the money is, but you are really drawn to interacting with people, you may want to reexamine your list of desires, which was the first step of the seven steps to using the Law of Attraction.

There are some good programs available to help you uncover your Life Purpose listed at the end of this book under Recommended Reading. If you have not already done so, I recommend looking into one of them. This will help you enhance your prosperity prospects. When your desires are aligned with your Life Purpose, things will begin to happen for you in a big way.

OMG! Yet another Exercise!

One technique many have found helpful is to **write your own obituary.**

When you have finished your business on this planet, what would you like to be remembered for?

Were you a teacher? A leader? A lover of fine art?

How long did you live? What legacy did you leave behind?

If you have any children, how were they influenced by you?

At your funeral, what would you like people to be saying when they recount their favorite memories of you?

Who misses you most and why?

It does not matter how long you lived; it matters how you lived.

How did you touch other people's lives?

How did you leave this planet in better shape than when you arrived?

Now write the longest, most eloquent obituary ever to run in the *New York Times* and make it all about what impressions you left behind. When you are done, consider what accomplishments not yet achieved that you can add to your list in the first step of using the Law of Attraction.

For example, if your future obituary states you were a marathon runner, yet you have not yet realized that goal, add "Run a marathon" to your list for the Law of Attraction to work on.

Last Exercise.

Now, after doing these exercises, you have the basis to write A Life Mission Statement. A Life Mission Statement states who you are, what you believe and who you will help. It is not a long document; typically one to three or four sentences at the most.

You can write your Life Mission Statement by taking the lists of likes and dislikes and the answers to the questions listed in the last exercise and extract the potent ideas and words.

> Writing or reviewing a mission statement changes you because it forces you to think through your priorities deeply, carefully, and to align your behavior with your beliefs. —Stephen Covey

Many powerful words you might use include *promote, empower, accomplish, write, produce, nurture, journey, encourage, impart, help, understand, give, inspire, integrate, understand, motivate, unite, guide, teach, enhance,* and so on.

For example, someone who is drawn to working with the soil may have a mission goal such as: *"I am an accomplished gardener who effortlessly grows high quality and nutritious produce from the soil I nurture for the benefit of human kind and the Planet Earth."*

A teacher may wish to affirm: *"I am a popular master motivator who nurtures and encourages the highest and best in all students who come into contact with me for their benefit and to benefit our growing society."*

Someone in the medical profession may like to use this mission statement: *"I am an accomplished healer who is striving to uncover the sources of diseases to affect a cure for the patients I serve and for human-kind worldwide."*

A person who likes to draw may have the mission statement of: *"I am a talented artist working in many media, whose works of art are appreciated by millions of people worldwide."*

I highly recommend the exercises in this chapter. Don't only do them once; go through them several times so you can refine your thoughts.

Now, pay attention to the results of the exercises.

For example, if your Mission Statements says you are solidly based in the earth as a farmer or forester, then you might wish to reconsider that desire to live on a houseboat in Tahiti.

When you are clear on your life mission, and you align your desires with that mission you will have gone a long way toward unlocking your Prosperity Code.

Key Number 8:
The Dreaded F Word!

This *F* Word" won't get a "Restricted" Rating from the Motion Picture Association of America. It won't get a child's mouth washed out with soap. It's not four letters long. It may not even rate a raised eyebrow, but I suspect that it will make you feel uncomfortable.

This word is "**Forgiveness**."

A good start in the process of forgiveness is what has been called Perceptual Cleaning. Our Mind has an attic which accommodates all kinds of disagreeable thoughts, emotions and attitudes. These may include envy, jealousy, rejection, fear, rage, revenge, addiction, resentment, anger, etc. They can be banished with a healthy dose of forgiveness. However unforgiveness holds them solidly in place and feeds their growth.

> Forgiveness is not an occasional act: it is a permanent attitude.
> —Martin Luther King, Jr.

Unforgiveness is the single most powerful barrier in the way of you realizing all that you are meant to be. Unforgiveness stunts spiritual growth and by doing so, it will stem the flow of prosperity from the Universe to you.

Unforgiveness is a burden you carry around. It may not feel like one, but it is there nonetheless. You are used to it. It is a part of you and your everyday make up. You do not remember when it was not there.

"Who *moi?*" you might be asking innocently now while polishing your halo and fluttering your eyelids. "I harbor no grudges!" So say you.

But wait.

One of my prosperity teachers told the story of a class in which the facilitator had each one of the students bring a clear plastic bag and a sack of potatoes. For every person they had refused to forgive in their life experience, they were told to choose a potato, write on it the name of the offender and the offense, and put it in the plastic bag. The size of the potato was to be in direct correlation to the perceived size of the affront. Some of their bags were very heavy.

> People can be more forgiving than you can imagine. But you have to forgive yourself. Let go of what's bitter and move on. —Bill Cosby

The students were told to carry this bag everywhere for a week, putting it next to their bed at night, on the car seat when driving, and close to their desk at school or work. The stress of carting it around with them made it clear the spiritual weight they were carrying. They also realized that they had to pay attention to it all the time to not forget or leave it in humiliating places.

Naturally, the condition of the potatoes deteriorated to a particularly unappetizing state. This was a great metaphor for the price they paid for keeping their pain and negativity and hauling it around with them. Too often we may think of forgiveness as a gift to the other person, but it clearly is for ourselves, my teacher told me.

So the next time you decide you can't forgive someone, ask yourself "Isn't my bag heavy enough?"

That is a great story and it graphically brings home the cost of unforgiveness.

There is another story of two especially devout Buddhist monks, one very senior and the other, fairly new. They lived an modest life, rarely dealing with the world outside their temple. One day, they were making their way on foot from their home temple to another for a meeting. Their route brought them to a river crossing. On the bank was a young woman of rather rentable virtue who asked to be carried across.

The elder monk without hesitation offered her his back and he carried her across. This unlikely behavior shocked the newbie and he was much troubled as they continued their journey. Finally, he could stand it no longer and said, "Venerable one, why did you stoop so low as to carry that unclean creature across the river?"

The older monk looked at him and said, "I put her down many miles back. Why have you have been carrying her ever since?"

Forgiveness begins at home. It starts in your own heart. **Many people find it relatively easy to forgive someone else, but they keep beating themselves up for something small.**

Judy, one of my students, came to me one day after class. "I did some forgiveness work last week," she said. "I was harboring some guilt about what I said to a dear friend years ago. I couldn't put it down and I had let our friendship go stale. So I called her and apologized. And do you know what she said?" Judy hesitated, and then continued. "She didn't have any memory of what had tormented me all these years, but she had been thinking about me and was going to call me! We're having lunch next week for the first time in three years!"

When you hear that inner voice of unforgiveness berating you for some petty thing, listen to it only long enough as to determine whose voice it is.

Is it a parent's voice? A sibling's? Another family member's? A teacher's? Stranger's? Friend's? Enemy's?

No matter whose voice it is, remember

> Holding on to anger is like grasping a hot coal with the intention of throwing it at someone; you are the one that gets burned.
> —Buddha

this: *They didn't know what they were talking about.* They were not in your skin or in your mind at the time, so they have no clue. In fact, they probably have no memory of the event or may even be gone from this planet.

I will acknowledge that there are certain individuals who live to criticize. I call these individuals *Irritant Personalities.* They grow by heaping guilt on others. What kind of a sad and unhappy life that is! You can recognize them for who they are and realize their way of life has no power over you.

One afternoon a few years ago, I took over a registration table at the beginning of a three-day spiritual conference and retreat, while the main organizer took a break. I was in the process of checking one person in when another woman came bustling up to the table and interrupted with a series of complaints. Her room wasn't right, the mattress was lumpy, the pillow had stains, there was no view and no air conditioner (which was hardly surprising, as this was in the mountains of North Carolina in early Fall) and so on.

In my head, I thought "Oh goody! Here is an Irritant Personality! I get to play with an Irritant Personality!" I assured the lady that I would be with her after I checked in the person in front of her.

When it was her turn, I was surprised to see that she had changed completely. Well, maybe the room wasn't quite so bad and perhaps the dining hall would have vegetarian meals and probably the weather would be nice. I assured her that everything was going to be all right, gave her some late breaking information and she went happily on her way. I saw her often in the next three days and she seemed to be having a great time.

What was different about that social transaction? Simply by my recognizing that she had that Irritant Personality I was able to have her transform her negative energy into something more positive. Irritants aren't always bad. Think of the irritant that is introduced into the pearl oyster; later it becomes a beautiful pearl. Irritants have their place in society: they help move things along.

Look at what happened when that Rabbi, who was born in Bethlehem, irritated the religious Powers That Be some two thousand years ago. He earned the scorn and hatred of those who had a stranglehold on the society at the time. They were not ready for his message of love and forgiveness. They were firmly rooted in the burning bush version of Jehovah. There was no room in

> For if you forgive men when they sin against you, your heavenly Father will also forgive you. But if you do not forgive men their sins, your Father will not forgive your sins. —Matthew 6:14-15

their precepts for love, clemency or mercy. What started as a societal irritant turned into a world-wide movement embracing that master's teachings.

When I give a talk, I like to use music during my lectures or services to reinforce my ideas. Master tunesmith Greg James helped me musically illustrate the benefits of forgiveness when he re-wrote the words of "Enjoy Yourself (It's Later Than You Think)" which were originally written by Herb Magidson in 1949.

All together now: Forgive Yourself

Forgive yourself, let love of self begin
Forgive yourself, for you're the best of friends
Be like the light pulled upward by the sun
Forgive yourself, and with yourself you're blessing everyone

That person in the mirror has been giving you some flack,
But when you start to frown at him you'll find he's frowning back
It's time that you forgive yourself for everything you do
And you will find that in your mind you're happier by two

Forgive yourself, let love of self begin
Forgive yourself, for you're the best of friends
Be like the light pulled upward by the sun
Forgive yourself, and with yourself you're blessing everyone

And when you start to criticize that you have missed the mark
Remember you're the keeper of the sacred holy spark
Your steps they may go front to back, they may go side to side
Cause life is not a ladder; it's a roller coaster ride!

Forgive yourself, let love of self begin
Forgive yourself, for you're the best of friends
Be like the light pulled upward by the sun
Forgive yourself, and with yourself you're blessing everyone

This story has a moral this forgiveness that you've found
Will fill the air like cinnamon and start to spread around
So remember when you bend a rule or break a shelf
It's all a part of living so just live forgive yourself

Forgive yourself, let love of self begin
Forgive yourself, for you're the best of friends
Be like the light pulled upward by the sun
Forgive yourself, and with yourself you're blessing everyone

(Now, give yourself a standing ovation!)

Forgiveness is a universal concept and need.

The concept of forgiveness is not only a Christian thing; it's a tenant of every major faith.

The Lord's Payer says "Forgive us our debts as we forgive the debts of others."

The Jewish tradition has the *Tefila Zaka* meditation, which is recited right before Yom Kippur, and closes with the following:"...I fully and finally forgive everyone; may no one be punished because of me. And just as I forgive everyone, so may You grant me grace in the eyes of others, that they too forgive me absolutely."

Islam teaches that God is "All-Forgiving."

Hindu priests intone: "O Lord, forgive three sins that are due to my human limitations: Thou art everywhere ... Lord, forgive three sins that are due to my human limitations."

Gandhi said: "Forgiveness is choosing to love. It is the first skill of self-giving love." When you learn to forgive and forgive sincerely, you will have cracked a major part of the Prosperity Code."

Bestselling author Colin Tipping developed *Radical Forgiveness*, a program which allows those who take it to accelerate the process of forgiveness in their lives. He developed the process while he was working with cancer patients. He determined that there was one thing in common among them: they had big knots of unforgiveness deep in their hearts. He used Radical Forgiveness as an easy and fast acting process for dissolving those knots. The tools simply dissolved the pain and left the participants peaceful, happy and in many cases, healed. The long-term benefits of Radical Forgiveness, according to Tipping, were better health, more energy, improved relationships, more prosperity, greater happiness, and a lot more peace in life.

If you dwell on insufficiency and limitations in your life, you are building a wall of lack that stops your abundance from flowing. **A regular practice of forgiveness will open the channels for your good to pour in.**

Key Number 9:
Have a Prosperity State of Mind

When you look at prosperity as closely as we have done in this book, you will discover that your job is not your source. Your family is not your source. Your winning lottery ticket is not your source. Your inheritance is not your source. Your source for your supply comes directly from the Creator. Whenever I write a check, I always write "**G I M S**" on the memo line. That reminds me that **G**od **I**s **M**y **S**ource, and there is *nothing else*. By acknowledging this Truth, you are dismantling your interior barriers to true prosperity.

Or to paraphrase comedian Richard Pryor: "Who are you going to believe: Truth or your lyin' eyes?"

Source may manifest as a paycheck or a lucky lottery ticket or a kind word from a stranger, but Source is *your* source of supply. If it doesn't manifest one way, it will manifest in another perhaps unexpected way. If one door closes, another will be opened to let Source shine through.

You may recall that when Moses asked who it was that was in the Burning Bush, God said "I AM that I am." Another name for God is "I AM".

Therefore when we say "I am poor" or "I am sick" or "I am not worthy", we are using Source's name to confirm our state of lack and limitation.

We make known the fact that we have been making these false beliefs real for ourselves and giving away our power to them. Speaking words of lack and limitation feeds these false concepts of our life, world and affairs. We are ruled by lies, metaphysically speaking, when we give *lack* and *limitation* the power of our words.

As we have said, you can think of the Universe as a huge copying machine. It you put negative thoughts into it, it will copy and return the negativity tenfold. If you put prosperity thoughts into it, you will get a ream of prosperity back.

Watch your words. When you find yourself berating yourself, stop. Reframe the thought. For example, if you hit your thumb, reframe the thought, "I am so clumsy!" into "There is a better way to do this that will not involve pain. I will do it that way from now on." Or, as noted earlier in this book, reframe "I can't afford that," into "*How* can I afford that?" Also consider "That's nice, and I have a different priority now." Always watch your words and reframe those negative thoughts into something more positive.

These habits of talking down about yourself may have developed from early childhood. **You did not come to this planet to fail. You came here to succeed and achieve your life goals.** These annoying habits have been dropped into your path to test your fortitude and resourcefulness. They can and will be overcome with the help of your Teammate.

You and God have been working as a team. You have clearly outlined your desire and cleaned out you mental closet of negative thoughts,

> The weak can never forgive. Forgiveness is the attribute of the strong. —Gandhi

attitudes, ideas and words. You have made space in your life for your abundance. You have visualized and projected yourself into the environment of your desires. You have watched your words and have set up a positive energy around your prosperity project.

Now give it a rest. Let God take over. Go take a walk or read a book or take a nap. Drop your project in God's "To Do" basket and walk away. Take a break. Go on vacation, even if it is to a city park.

When you are cooking something in your microwave, don't stand in front of it and yell "Hurry Up!" Most people will let the microwave do what it is supposed to do.

Let the Universe do what *it* is supposed to do: bring you your richly deserved abundance.

Act with honesty, cooperation and justice when dealing with God and with those around you. Be ethical in your thoughts, words and deeds. Some spiritual people see their fathers and mothers as the human instruments through which they are provided with a body, and nurtured until they can make their way in the world without outside human help. Through honoring your father and mother, you are also honoring God as Source of all that is. You can consider the entire population of this planet as your fathers and mothers, brothers and sisters, sons and daughters. They are, in a way, your global family.

The Pond of Prosperity

A pond must have three things to be called a pond: First, it must have water. Then it has to have a way for the water to get in. Finally it has to have someplace for the water to exit. What happens if the entrance and exit is dammed up? The water in the pond becomes stagnant and foul. Nothing good emanates from it.

The stagnant pond is the metaphor for what happens when you hold on to your wealth and refuse to reinvest it in your growing abundance. If you are as avaricious as Scrooge McDuck and his bottomless swimming pool of gold and jewels, you have no room in your heart and soul to make your good work for the betterment of those around you.

Several of the United States' richest people have committed to giving away a good part of their wealth. The blessings they confer will help untold numbers of people realize their ambitions to have a home, or go to school or to even have a meal on the table.

When something pure has been spoiled by the introduction of a malicious or a nasty foreign or an inferior substance, it has been adulterated. What was supposed to be pure has been debased. This process not only happens in relationships and in chemistry but also in the Spiritual realm of prosperity.

There are numerous true stories of people who were fortunate enough to win a large sum of money in the lottery, to the tune of a million dollars or more. They went from living in a rented trailer to living in a Beverly Hillbillies Mansion. They traded their elderly smog belcher in for two, three or more brand new sports cars and flashy SUVs. They found that their circle of "friends" had grown exponentially. People were always flocking around them, usually with their hands outstretched. They were rich and popular.

> If you're doing something you love, you're more likely to put your all into it, and that generally equates to making money.—Warren Buffett

And they were unhappy.

But they couldn't change their poverty mentality to a prosperity mentality.

Within a year, their friends had fled, their houses and cars were repossessed and they often found themselves living in dire straits. Again.

Why? Because when they received their bounty from the Universe, they did not accept it in the spiritual sense that it was offered. They debased the purity of the gift.

Does this mean that when you have your Abundance that you can't buy a new house, car, vacation or wardrobe? Of course not. The simple action of thanking Spirit and returning to the Universe a tithe will continue to magnify and multiply your Abundance.

Have you ever looked at someone who has been unethical or illegal in his activities and asked: "How did that fool ever become so rich when I'm here barely making it?"

The answer lies in your respective states of mind. The unethical person may at first seem to be richly blessed, but you will never know what inner demons are being battled. Your state of mind, on the other hand, may be locked into a poverty complex. By following the instructions in this book, you will unlock the Prosperity Code and surge far ahead of the other person. They will also have to face their individual judgment day with regards to their unsavory activities.

If you are not generous to life, life will not be generous to you.

Emerson sums it up in his essay entitled *Compensation*. "Every man takes care that his neighbor shall not cheat him. But a day comes when he begins to care that he does not cheat his neighbor. Then all goes well. He has changed his market cart into a chariot of the sun."

When you acknowledge God as your source, you are refusing to acknowledge the power of lack and limitation and poverty. (Recall my habit of writing God Is My Source or GIMS on my checks). You are free of fear of lack because of God's presence in, and through, all that you are and do.

> There's enough for everyone. If you believe it, if you can see it, if you act from it, it will show up for you. That's the truth. —Rev. Michael Beckwith

When something is coveted, the result is inevitably a failure to look to God as our source of supply.

Allow me to give a personal example. Once I was up for what I thought was the perfect job working for a regional sports telecasting company. I was one of two finalists. However, the other person got the job. I really wanted the position so I prayed that the successful candidate would find a better job and move elsewhere. In other words I coveted the job.

Two days after I started my prayer process, I received a phone call from the HR Manager at the company. The other person had been forced to resign to move out of the city, and would I still be interested in coming to work for them?

I excitedly agreed to take the position. Later that same day, I received a request to work on a short term project for another company that could have the potential of turning into a long-term and full-time highly compensated position. I told the caller that I couldn't help him because I had taken the sports job.

When I showed up for my first day, I discovered that it was a contract position and that the contract could be nullified by the company without notice. Because I really wanted the job, and because the pay was good, I signed the contract and started to work.

That first week, I found out that the first candidate had been forced to resign because his father was dying of cancer and he had to return to his family home to care for him. Not what I would have wished for him: I wanted him to get a better job. Strike one.

The second week I worked there, I discovered the job was all about office politics. I don't do office politics, but it was a way of life in this company. It is my firm belief that someone is hired to do a job and not to be unduly subservient to the moods of certain people in an office or company. Strike two.

The last week I showed up for work, I discovered that I no longer had an office. The space I had been using had been given to someone else and I was relegated to an empty desk sitting in a storage area. Strike three.

Shortly thereafter, I asked to be released from my contract. And I gladly left one of the worst jobs I have ever had.

By coveting a job that was rightfully another's, I limited the good that I could receive. I turned down an opportunity that could have been very positive for me in my career path at the time to take the job I coveted.

When we forget God has all that is good for us, we short circuit God's energy flowing through our faith toward manifesting our desired outcome. We interfere with the spiritual force on its way to manifestation.

When another is prosperous, sincerely rejoice in their good. Do not denigrate or belittle their gain. Adding your energy to theirs will redouble your prosperity energy to manifest your Abundance even quicker than before.

Affirm: "I am a child of God. I can do all things through His power which strengthens me."

Key Number 10:
Have A Regular Spiritual Practice

||||||||||||||||||||||||||||||||||||||||||||||||||||||||||||||||||||||||||||||||||||||||||||||||||||||||||||||||||||||||||

I f you want your prosperity energy to increase, you must meet it part way. When your abundance vibrations increase, the vibrations in the rest of your life must of necessity also increase. This is why this key to the code includes a proactive regular spiritual practice.

Prayer and meditation are the two vital parts of a regular spiritual practice.

Praying is where you talk and Source listens.

Meditation is where Source talks and you keep your mouth shut and mind open.

As noted earlier, we are always praying subconsciously. Our thoughts form the litany of prayers about our life, traffic, family, relationships, work and weight, among millions of other things.

In your Conscious Prayer time, you will have the opportunity to focus your prayers for the good of yourself and for others. Note the word "good." If you use your prayer time to pray for something bad to happen to another, then you may very well find yourself hip deep in dire circumstances and anxiety.

Here is an example of praying for the good of all concerned: Bradley had a challenge with the barking of a neighbor's dog. For whatever reason, the neighbor and the dog refused any conscious entreaties to have quiet time while he was sleeping. Brad had recently been introduced to the concept of Conscious Prayer in one of my classes.

In his regular spiritual practice time, he prayed that the dog finds canine bliss in being quiet during the night. He visualized the dog sleeping quietly from sundown to sun up. He prayed that the dog's previously uncooperative owner would realize the problem and bring the dog inside at night. Finally, he prayed that the sound of the dog's bark would no longer disturb his sleep, unless it meant a danger to him and his family.

He prayed these Conscious Prayers without any negative emotions attached to them. He sent the dog and its owner the love and peace of the Creator.

After a week of these prayers, Bradley reported that he was no longer bothered by the barking. In fact, he said, he had to look into his neighbor's yard to be sure the dog was still there. The dog was still there but the ability of its bark to annoy him had left.

You can use Conscious Prayer every day in your life for things more important than a vocal pooch. You can pray for the improved health of a loved one. You can pray for an improved relationship, whether on the personal level or in the workplace. You can pray for your family, community or world.

Conscious Prayer works for those for whom you are praying. But most importantly, it works for you. Like love, you can't give it away without getting some on yourself.

Look at it as practicing the Presence of God.

The second part of your regular spiritual practice is Meditation.

With meditation, you shut down the monkey thoughts in your head and listen for that still, small voice.

Monkey thoughts are those thoughts which attempt to distract you from your meditation: my nose itches, my leg is asleep, what if the kids make noise, how will I do everything I need to do today, I don't have time for this, etc.

What do you do with monkey thoughts? Recognize them for what they are and put them away. This will take some practice, but after a few times, it will become second nature.

Your regular spiritual practice needs to be engaged twice a day: upon arising and shortly before retiring. Why then? If you meditate upon arising, you are setting the intentions for your day at a deep level of mind. When you meditate before going to sleep, you are sleeping on, and strengthening, your desires for a better life.

How to meditate.

There are many different techniques for meditation. When you master this basic technique, you may wish to fold in some variations of your own.

This particular technique does not require you to vocalize a specific sound such as "Om." Instead you mentally say your mantra. A mantra is a word or sound mentally repeated to facilitate concentration. Initially, try using the mantra "God Is Love" for your meditation. Think "God Is" when you inhale and "Love" when you exhale. Allow yourself to be absorbed in the words. Don't force it. Let it come easily and naturally.

Sit comfortably in a quiet place when you begin. When you become a seasoned meditator, you will be able to meditate in the middle of Grand Central Station at rush hour. There is no need for a "special" sitting position. If sitting on the floor with your legs crossed is uncomfortable, then find another way or another place to sit which won't distract your mind from the purpose of meditation.

Close your eyes. Breathe naturally and easily. Sit for about a minute to allow your breathing and heart to slow down from your day. Keep your spine straight, head balanced. Avoid meditating in a supine position unless you want to fall asleep.

Some people like to engage in a relaxation routine before fully meditating. They visualize every part of their body from the skin on their scalp to the tips of their toes and all the parts between as having increased relaxation and less tension. They feel the tension leaving the selected part of their body and feel relaxation enveloping them piece by piece.

Pay attention to your breath and breathe gently and easily. Most people find it helpful to use the "God Is Love" Mantra to do this.

Allow your monkey thoughts and feelings to come and go with indifference.

You do not have to control them in any way. You only have to recognize them for what they are, and when you realize you are not repeating the "God Is Love" mantra, gently return to it. You don't need to force yourself to think the mantra to the exclusion of everything else.

Meditate in this way for about 15 minutes. It is acceptable to glance at a clock or to set a quiet vibration ring tone on your smart phone to time your meditation. Above all, do not use an intrusive alarm such as a kitchen timer. You may experience a deep state of relaxation, but it is perfectly normal if you do not when starting out as a mediator. Stay with it. Don't give up. One day, you will come out of a deep meditation without realizing you had actually entered it.

When you are done, take some time to slowly return to normal awareness. Be gentle with yourself when opening your eyes or getting up after a meditation. To get up quickly after the state of deep rest that is often a result of meditation can cause what I call "Spiritual Whiplash," until you are able to program yourself to come back from meditating easily and naturally.

Many people like to pray or do visualization after meditating, while still in an altered state. The Silva Life Systems method uses this higher level state of mind for spiritual work. Founder José Silva discovered that the brain wave frequencies in the meditative state allow for healing and renewal, among many other positive things. When you operate at this level of mind, good things will happen.

During this level of meditation, you may be able to receive insights into the solution of any problems you may be facing.

Thomas Edison knew this fact. His lab was equipped with a comfortable cot and he would take cat naps in order to receive inspired ideas. His technique included lying down with some steel ball bearings loosely cupped in one hand. As he entered the space of REM (Rapid Eye Movement) that accompany deep relaxation and dreaming, he would often get some of his best ideas. As he fell deeper asleep, his hand would relax and the steel balls would fall to the floor, awakening him while the memory of his dream was still fresh in his mind.

You can use your meditative state not only to listen to your inner guidance, but also to visualize yourself in a state of Abundance, as suggested in the chapter on the Law of Abundance.

The ultimate purpose of a regular spiritual practice is to insert your mind into the natural flow and vibration of Abundance and to extricate your thoughts from the paths of Lack and Limitation.

First time meditator Jane said "Spend 30 minutes meditating and praying when I could just as easily be sleeping? You've got to be kidding!" Yet, after engaging in meditation for only five days, she was surprised to discover her regular spiritual practice actually allowed her to have *more* time instead of less during the day.

"Spending a mere 30 minutes a day in prayer and meditation," Jane told me later, "allowed me to focus on things important to my increasing my Abundance, and discard things that aren't in line with that goal. I was amazed that I found myself with more time to do the things I really wanted to do!" Jane's coworkers are used to the fact that she can often be found meditating before she undertakes a large project.

The regular practice of meditation will help you smooth out the ups and downs of the day, gain more insight into your spiritual self and open the gates of Abundance to flood you with good.

Key Number 11:
Examine And Modify
Your Core Values.

Y our Core Values are the constant elements in your ever-changing life. Your core values govern your personal relationships. If you are in business, your business core values define the ethics of your company. Your core values require no external justification and are the essential tenants that rule your life. They are practices to use every day in everything you do in your life.

Since your core values articulate what you stand for and guide you in making decisions, they underpin your whole being. By examining and modifying your core values, you will have mastered a major key in unlocking the Prosperity Code.

The first and most important Core Value is the value you place on money.

What does money represent to you? Is it a source of trouble, strife and anxiety? Is it the Be-All and End-All of your life? Is amassing stacks and stacks of money the proverbial carrot that keeps you plodding from one financial disaster to another? Is money an addiction like the common addictions to alcohol, tobacco, food, sex or shoes?

Do you find yourself dodging bill collectors, putting off paying credit cards and asking for advances as a regular form of behavior?

If this in any way describes your life now, you may be what Julia Cameron and Mark Bryan call "A Money Drunk," in their 1992 book *Money Drunk/Money Sober.*

As mentioned briefly in an earlier chapter, money is only a symbol. That printed piece of paper has a very low intrinsic value. *We* give money its power, and as such, *we* can take that spin off it.

Your first step is to recognize that you have an undue amount of energy attached to money. You are giving your power away to it. The movie *Wall Street* had Gordon Gekko affirming "Greed is good." Greed, or more correctly avarice, is the jumping off point for a wide variety of personal, social and spiritual ills. Greed causes many people to act out with their money. Being addicted to money causes ruined relationships, lost jobs and personal turmoil.

Look closely at your relationship to money. If you are feeling any kind of negative energy, start by recording every cent that comes in and every cent that goes out. (There are many excellent personal finance programs available to do this on your computer.)

Once you see that you may be spending more than you make or spending money faster than it comes in, defuse that situation by accepting it and working to change it.

An excellent method of changing your attitude is through some of the self-care affirmations listed earlier in this book. I have to remind you that this process is not about punishing yourself. This process is about healing yourself.

You can try one of these affirmations:

Money is my friend. It helps me but does not rule me. Money has no power over my life.

I accept money in an easy manner, knowing that I can easily save it for long term use.

Money is attracted to me easily and effortlessly.

Money is happy to be with me and I am happy to be with money, because I know it has no power over me.

Money

Core Value: I accept the Divine blessings of abundance in my life and family now. I accept for myself and all humanity an abundance of prosperity, health, peace, joy and financial evolution.

And so it is.

Now, let's examine a few other more esoteric core values and see if they resonate.

Love

Core Value: *I express unconditional love, an inner quality that sees goodness everywhere and in everyone.*

How can you express this value? You can actively and passively express love in the world.

You can welcome and greet everyone in love.

Merely by smiling at people and mentally blessing them, you activate this value.

You can look for the good in others and speak well of others (i.e.: shun gossiping.)

You can be considerate of others and listen with empathy.

You can practice non-judgment and forgiveness (see the Chapter on the Dreaded "F" Word).

Spirit

Core value: *I turn within and am directed by Spirit in all I do.*

You create harmony, peace and order in yourself and others when you align your daily actions with spiritual principles. There is only one Presence and one Power in your life, world and affairs.

> Let your Self be One with something beyond it. — *A Course in Miracles*

You practice this core value by having a daily practice that keeps you conscious of Spirit. This practice uses prayer, affirmations and meditation to connect with Spirit and nourishes your soul.

You can attend classes and workshops that support your spiritual growth.

Incorporate life's challenges and celebrations into your daily prayers. As life presents you with opportunities, you center yourself using your spiritual practices.

Inclusiveness

Core value: *I am One connected with All.* You may think of yourself as an individual, but realize that on the soul level you are connected with the Universe.

To use this core value, you see each person as an expression of God, even though you may not agree with their opinions or their behaviors. You are considerate of all and have compassion for everyone.

In addition, you take opportunities to be exposed to different faiths and cultures, while recognizing them as part of Spirit. You participate in activities that increase your understanding of all people.

To help support this planet, you reduce, reuse and recycle to create a sustainable world.

Joy

Core value: *I live from a positive view of the world and celebrate life.* Joy is your true nature. You celebrate your oneness with God through laughter, fun and playfulness. Singing is like praying twice, so sing, even if it is in the shower.

You use this core value by choosing to be optimistic and filled with joy. You appreciate humor wherever you find it, be it out of the mouth of a child or a sophisticated cartoon in *The New Yorker*.

You live in the consciousness of gratitude with your awareness of your connection to all life.

Integrity

Core value: *I adhere to my values and have the awareness and courage to act accordingly to those values.* You act from a place of wholeness and are ethical in all your actions.

Don Miguel Ruiz's classic book *The Four Agreements* speaks very closely to this core.

His first Agreement says "Be impeccable with your word." Say what you mean and speak in integrity. Use the power of your word to speak your truth and reject gossip either from others or from yourself.

The second Agreement is "Don't take anything personally." Nothing others do is because of you. When you are immune from their misguided statements and opinions, nothing can bring you down.

The third Agreement is "Don't make assumptions." Ask questions and express what you want. Open communication with others to negate misunderstandings, drama and sadness.

The final Agreement is "Always do your best." Strive for excellence, not perfection. A perfectionist doesn't finish a job, he just abandons it. By doing your best, you will avoid regret and self-judgment.

By aligning yourself to these core values, you will have gone a long way spiritually as well as toward manifesting your rightful Abundance.

Solving the Code:
Putting it all Together

N ow, it's time to take everything discussed so far in this book, and put them all together to unlock the Prosperity Code for *yourself.*

If you have been paying attention and doing the exercises, you will find this to be a snap. Perhaps I have challenged several long-held beliefs and habits. For some, this may have been a long and demanding journey. But ask yourself:

Aren't you ready to change?

Let us first review the eleven basic keys:

> To me, true prosperity begins with feeling good about yourself. It is also the freedom to do what you want to do, when you want to do it. It is never an amount of money; it is a state of mind. Prosperity or lack of it is an outer expression of the ideas in your head. —Louise L. Hay

Key Number 1: What is Prosperity?
In this chapter, you made your own definition of prosperity. You completed the statement "I feel prosperous when…"

Key Number 2: What Are You Asking From The Universe?

What is it exactly that you are asking of the Universe? Are you placing an order for peace, love and abundance or are you asking for upset, anxiety and anger? What kind of Mind-set do you have: a Scarcity mind-set or an Abundance mind-set?

Key Number 3: What Are Universal Laws And How Do They Affect Me?

The Law of Abundance is only one interrelated with other Universal Spiritual Laws. By seeing these Laws and understanding how they work, you can take advantage of their precepts to manifest your Abundance.

Key Number 4: The Seven Steps to Using the Law of Attraction.

The seven steps include "Create," "Focus," "Act," "Move," "Let Go," "Give Thanks" and "Receive". Using these seven simple steps in an orderly and applied manner will go a long way toward unlocking the Prosperity Code.

Key Number 5: Have Faith and Believe.

When you believe that *Abundance* is you birthright, your destiny, your purpose here in this life, you will unlock another portion of the Prosperity Code.

Key Number 6: To Receive, You Must Also Give.

The Universe returns to you what you give out blessed and multiplied. What are you giving out? Is it stress and worry or is it joy and abundance?

Key Number 7: Are You in Line With Your Life's Purpose?

If you did the exercises in this chapter, you will have a better idea of your life's purpose. You will have developed a Life Mission Statement which you will use to align your desires with your mission.

Key Number 8: Forgiveness is Necessary to Move Forward in Life.

The major block to receiving your abundance is a lack of forgiveness and gratitude. All your experiences thus far in life have made you what you are. Be grateful for them and let them go.

Key Number 9: Have A Prosperity State of Mind.

Concentrate on your good and watch your words. Remember that the thoughts you hold dear will manifest. Be sure you desire those thoughts.

Key Number 10: Have A Regular Spiritual Practice.

If you want your prosperity energy to increase, then you must meet it part way. When your Abundance vibrations increase, the vibrations in the rest of your life must of necessity also increase. This is why this key includes a proactive regular spiritual practice to turbocharge your abundance transformation.

Key Number 11: Examine and modify your core values.

Your core values are the constant elements in your ever-changing life. Your core values govern your personal relationships. If you are in business, your business core values define the ethics of your company. **Your core values require no external justification.** They are the essential tenants that rule your life. They are practices to use every day in everything you do.

If you followed the instructions and completed the exercises in this book, you should be able to check off the following:

- I have a clear picture of what being prosperous means to me. I know how it feels, what it looks like and what it means for myself, my loved ones and society.
- I have examined my conscious and unconscious prayer life and removed any negative prayers and thoughts that are detrimental to my prosperity. I have substituted positive and beneficial statements in their places.

- I am familiar with the Universal Laws and know how they affect me, my life, my world and my affairs. I align my thoughts and actions with these laws.
- I have followed the Seven Steps to Using the Law of Attraction.
- I have made my vision board. I view it and send it positive energy every day.
- I have a clear vision of my prosperity and I hold to that vision or something better.
- I have faith in the Universe that I will experience Abundance. I am stepping back and letting my teammate God do the heavy lifting.
- I acknowledge that to receive, I must also give. I tithe to my source of spiritual nourishment. I also give of my time and my talents. I know all that I give will be returned to me blessed and multiplied a hundred times over.
- I have completed the exercises to get a feeling of the purpose of my life. I have aligned my prosperity desires with that purpose and realize Abundance will come to me much more quickly.
- I have forgiven myself, and I have forgiven those whom I deemed to have hurt or injured me. I realize I cannot receive my true Abundance until there is no more unforgiveness in my heart.
- I have a prosperity state of mind. My words, thoughts and actions are positive and aimed toward universal abundance for all.
- I have established, and I follow, a regular spiritual practice. The time spent in prayer and meditation adds to my life and my prosperity. I have plenty of time to do all that I have to do and do it well.
- I have determined and reviewed my core values. I know that my values of love, spirit, joy, inclusiveness and integrity serve me as well as the world around me to the best and highest good for all.

Congratulations! You have broken the Prosperity Code!

It's time for you to undertake and complete this passage. Meet the challenges. Rise to the task. Ignore the naysayers and keep your faith focused on your goal of abundance.

Stay in touch. Let me know how you are doing. I want to hear your stories. Contact me at www.ProsperityCodeToday.com and share your successes!

You may be surprised at your results, but I won't.

I have faith in you, just as God does.

Finally, let me remind you that God has your picture on His refrigerator.

The End

Recommended Reading

T his is a small list of books which I have read over the years and they have been very helpful in unlocking the Prosperity Code for me.

They are available for on-line ordering, but please do not neglect the brick and mortar and independently-owned book sellers if you have a choice. These merchants, too, are providing you with spiritual nourishment.

Browne, Sylvia, *Life on the Other Side,* NAL Trade, 2002

Butterworth, Eric, *Spiritual Economics*, Unity Press, 1993

Chopra, Deepak, *The Seven Spiritual Laws of Success,* Amber-Allen Publishing, 1994

Foundation for Inner Peace, *A Course in Miracles*, Viking Penguin, 1996

Gaines, Edwene, *The Four Spiritual Laws of Prosperity,* Rodale Books, 2005

Hay, Louise L., *Receiving Prosperity*, (Audio CD) Hay House Publishing, 2005

Hay, Louise L., *You Can Heal Your Life,* Hay House Publishing, 2008

Lamsa, George, *The Holy Bible from The Ancient Eastern Text*, (trans.) Harper Collins, 1985

Millman, Dan, *The Life You Were Born to Live: A Guide to Finding Your Life Purpose*, H J Kramer, 1993

Newton, Michael Ph.D. *Journey of Souls*, Llewellyn Publications, 1994

Ponder, Catherine; *The Dynamic Laws of Prosperity*, BN Publishing, 1985

Ponder, Catherine, *Open Your Mind to Prosperity*, DeVorss Publications, 1984

Price, John Randolph, *The Abundance Book and 40 Day Prosperity Plan*, Quartus Books, 1987

Smith, Stretton, *The 4T Prosperity Program,* The 4T Publishing Company, 2011

Tipping, Colin, *Radical Forgiveness,* Sounds True Publishing, 2009

Toll, Eckhart, *Finding Your Life's Purpose,* Penguin, 2008

West, Georgiana Tree, *Prosperity's Ten Commandments*, Unity Press, 1996

Afterword

S tay in touch and share your prosperity stories. Go to www. ProsperityCodeToday.com and check out the latest affirmations, prosperity thoughts and Alan Batten's blog postings. Become a part of the world-wide Prosperity Code Community. Share your excitement and triumphs with everyone on the web!

CPSIA information can be obtained at www.ICGtesting.com
Printed in the USA
BVOW022302250712

296201BV00003B/46/P

9 781452 552675